The Canadian Garden Cookbook

Jennifer Sayers • James Darcy

The Canadian Garden Cookbook

First Printing June 2014

Library and Archives Canada Cataloguing in Publication

Sayers, 1975-, author

The Canadian garden cookbook / Jennifer Sayers, James Darcy.

(Canada cooks series)

Includes index.

Originally published: Edmonton : Lone Pine Publishing, 2009

ISBN 978-1-927126-70-7 (pbk.)

1. Cooking, Canadian. 2. Cooking (Fruit). 3. Cooking (Vegetables).

4. Cookbooks. I. Darcy, James, author II. Title. III. Series: Canada cooks series

TX715.6.B346 2014   641.5971   C2014-900820-1

Cover image: Stuffed Pepper © Pawe Strykowski / Photos.com; Stuffed Tomatoes © ivanmateev / Photos.com
Photo p. 7: Photos.com

Published by

Company's Coming Publishing Limited

87 East Pender Street,
Vancouver, BC, Canada V6A 1S9

Tel: 604-687-5555   Fax: 604-687-5575

www.companyscoming.com

Company's Coming is a registered trademark owned by Company's Coming Publishing Limited

We acknowledge the financial support of the Government of Canada through the Canada Book Fund for our publishing activities.

Printed in China

PC: 21

CONTENTS

ACKNOWLEDGEMENTS

Special thanks to Chris, my little apprentice Diego and my friend
Tracy Waritsky. Thanks also to photographers Sandy Weatherall
and Nanette Samol, Alison Beck, Lone Pine and Gwendolyn
Simpson, grower of herbs and edible flowers extraordinaire.

INTRODUCTION

Since the beginnings of human civilization, gardening and cooking have gone hand in hand. As humans began to cultivate crops, we learned increasingly complex cooking techniques. In Canada, most of us no longer have to grow the food we eat, but as our awareness of the food we eat increases, more and more of us are returning to the idea of culinary gardens. Some of us grow an edible garden because we love to garden, some of us to save money, some of us to help protect the environment and some of us to have a ready supply of a wider variety of produce. Whatever the reason we plant it, we all enjoy eating the fruits of our labour at harvest time.

Depending on where in Canada you live, you may have to work a little harder at growing certain edibles. We certainly won't be growing mangoes in the backyard any time soon, but there is a cornucopia of other foods that can be grown in Canadian gardens. Even if you don't have abundant space for a large vegetable garden, you can still grow some of your own edibles. Choose a few favourites to plant in containers on a patio or balcony and buy the rest from the farmers' market for produce that's nearly as fresh as home-grown.

We can learn a lot about cooking from a season in the garden. Plants that grow well together often taste even better together, like the classical pairing of tomatoes with basil. In the garden, basil helps protect tomatoes from pests, while in the kitchen basil's mild licorice scent is a perfect accompaniment for tomatoes' bright savoury flavour. Plants from the same family also tend to have complementary flavours, like tomatoes and

eggplants, which appear together in many dishes. Observing the shapes and colours of our food as it grows can provide inspiration for new dishes and pairings and helps to remind us that we eat with our eyes first.

Growing and eating our own vegetables and fruits also helps to remind us that most produce was once strictly seasonal. Much as we might enjoy eating asparagus all year long, it simply tastes better in the spring, and still better when paired with other seasonal ingredients as a celebration of the season. Following the chronology of our gardens helps us enjoy the growing season; time seems to move more slowly when counted in peas, asparagus, potatoes, tomatoes, peppers and squash than when counted in days, weeks and months.

As gardeners, we enjoy the time we spend in the garden, tending to the soil and the plants, spotting first the flowers, then the tiny green fruits. But the ultimate reward is the fruit itself. That burst of flavour as you pop the first of the season's strawberries into your mouth, the juices of a garden-ripened tomato running down your chin—this is what we look forward to all season.

We've come up with more than 70 recipes featuring the most common veggies, herbs and fruit grown in gardens across Canada; especially popular or prolific plants get a second recipe, for good measure. Some of the recipes are twists on familiar classics, others are meant to make you see your garden favourites in a new light. But all of them

try to preserve that fresh-from-the-garden flavour. While the recipes don't always use a great quantity of the central ingredient, it is essential to the character of each recipe, the thing that makes the dish. For the most part, the recipes are simple because when the food you're cooking is that fresh, you simply don't want to do too much to it; you want the flavours to sing, bright and clear.

You won't be able to find all the ingredients for these recipes in your garden. The rest of your ingredients should be of the best quality you can get, so they don't bring your garden-fresh ingredients down. Consult the remaining sections of the Introduction for our recommendations on essential ingredients and techniques.

Note that we've organized the recipes alphabetically by what is grown in the garden.

If you need a great garden book to accompany this cookbook, look no further than Alison Beck's *The Canadian Edible Garden* (Lone Pine Publishing, 2008). It is organized in the same order as the recipes here, and can be used to increase your knowledge and appreciation of a culinary garden tucked in among your other plants.

In Our Kitchen

We have found the following ingredient choices and cooking procedures to be successful in our kitchen and recommend them highly wherever possible.

Butter is unsalted and is easiest to measure using the convenient markings on the wrapping. Before you cut, be sure to check that the outer markings are aligned with the ends of the block of butter.

Citrus juices are fresh squeezed.

Eggs are large, free-range eggs. They should be at room temperature for baking. If you forget to pull your eggs out of the refrigerator, you can speed up the warming by placing them, uncracked, in a bowl of warm water.

Flour is unbleached all-purpose.

Herbs are fresh, unless stated otherwise. In a pinch, the best alternative to fresh is frozen. To prolong the herb harvest from your garden, mince herbs and place in ice cube forms with a little water to cover, then freeze. Once frozen, they can be transferred to freezer bags to bring fresh summer flavour to winter dishes.

Mushrooms, such as morels and chanterelles, can be found in the wild, but we advise that you confirm the identification of mushrooms with an experienced collector before cooking them; some species are acutely toxic and can cause death.

Stocks are homemade. Good quality stocks in cans or aseptic boxes are the best substitute. Avoid using those nasty little cubes or powders. Miso, a fermented soybean paste, makes an interesting alternative to stock. It will keep in the refrigerator for several months. Stir it in 1 Tbsp (15 mL) at a time until you have a rich, full flavour.

Sugar is organic and unrefined rather than white and bleached. When looking for a rich brown sugar, use muscovado sugar, available in grocery and health food stores. It retains the minerals and vitamins originally in the sugar cane plant, and it has a full molasses flavour.

Yeast is regular dry yeast; 1/2 oz (15 mL) dry yeast is equal to 1 Tbsp (15 mL) fresh yeast.

Essential Ingredients

The following ingredients are used in many of the recipes in this book; special ingredients found in just one or two recipes are described where they are used. Some items are widely available, whereas others are best sought in gourmet, specialty food, health food or ethnic stores or obtained by mail order or the Internet.

Bay Leaves—Fresh leaves have such a different flavour that they are worth the effort to find. They are occasionally available at large grocery stores and can be specially ordered. In a well-sealed container in the fridge, they can last three or four months.

Coconut Milk—Use unsweetened coconut milk in cans. Naturally sweet, it is often better than cream in savoury dishes.

Garlic—Use fresh! An Italian friend once told me that if you can't be bothered to peel and chop fresh garlic, you shouldn't be allowed to use it!

Lemons and Limes—Use fresh! You can't compare the taste to concentrate.

Mayonnaise—It's always better homemade:

5 egg yolks

2/3 cup (150 mL) extra virgin olive oil

1/4 cup (60 mL) good quality vinegar or juice from 1 lemon

pinch of sea salt to taste

- You need both hands free to make mayonnaise. Spread a damp cloth on your counter, nestle a medium-sized bowl in its centre and wrap the cloth around the base of the bowl to keep it steady while you whisk.

- Whisk yolks, vinegar and salt in bowl until well combined and yolks have lightened in colour.

- Add oil, a drop at a time, whisking continuously until mixture emulsifies and thickens.

- When about half of oil has been added, whisk in remaining oil in a slow, steady stream. Store, covered, in refrigerator for up to five days. You can thin your mayonnaise by lightly whisking in some water.

- Many people like to add mustard or fresh herbs to their mayonnaise. Adding minced garlic turns plain mayonnaise into aïoli. Makes just over 1 cup (250 mL).

Mustard—Use good quality mustard for everything from sandwiches to dressings to sauces. When you are down to the last few teaspoons clinging to the bottom of your mustard jar, add fresh lemon juice, olive oil, sea salt and fresh pepper for a yummy impromptu salad dressing. Just shake and enjoy.

Oil, Grape Seed—Grape seed oil has a very light flavour and can be heated to very high temperatures without smoking or burning. These qualities make it ideal for sautéing, frying and oven roasting.

Oil, Olive—Extra virgin olive oil is indispensable. Good olive oils have fantastic, robust flavour, but burn easily. Use extra virgin olive oil for salad dressings, mayonnaise and other cold recipes, or splashed into a sauce at the end of cooking for a little flavour, but do not use it for cooking. Try olive oil from Italy, Spain or Greece.

Oil, Sesame—Use for a nutty flavour addition. Store it in the fridge.

Pepper, Fresh—Freshly ground pepper has a far superior flavour to pre-ground, which loses a lot of its pungency and spice. A variety of peppercorns are available; try some of the multi-coloured pepper blends for a slightly different flavour, but do not substitute white pepper for black.

Peppers—When handling hot peppers, wear plastic or rubber gloves to avoid capsaicin burns. Capsaicin is the compound in all varieties of pepper (except bell peppers) that gives them their heat, and it is easily transferred through skin-to-skin contact. If you decide to live dangerously and forego the gloves, make sure you wash your hands thoroughly before touching your face, eyes or loved ones.

Salt—Great salt is the key to great cooking. Salt brings out the flavour in food. There are many amazing salts in the world to reach for—sea salt, kosher salt or flavoured salts—choose a favourite. Better yet, obtain some of each. Remember that salt can have a chemical aftertaste, and using a better quality salt also means that you will use less, because the flavour is more intense. If you need to reduce salt even further for health reasons, use fresh herbs, various spices and flavour lifters such as lemon juice to maintain the intensity while reducing the salt content.

Soy Sauce—Both tamari and shoyu are high-quality, fermented and chemical-free sauces that are used to enhance flavour and impart a unique saltiness.

Vinegar, Apple Cider—Use when you need an all-purpose vinegar; organic, unrefined and unpasteurized apple cider vinegar has the best flavour.

Vinegar, Balsamic—Its unique flavour is great in everything from soups to sweets.

A Final Note on Measuring

Dry ingredients should be spooned into the measuring cup and levelled off with a knife or spatula.

Solids, including butter and most cheeses, are measured in dry-measure cups and liquids in liquid-measure cups.

Amaranth Breakfast Cereal with Maple, Lemon and Berries

Serves 4

Amaranth is both beautiful to grow, with its bright flowers and often bicoloured foliage, and delicious to eat. In this dish, we've cooked the seeds into a warm breakfast cereal, but if you change up the seasonings, you can use the same method and serve them hot as a side dish or cold as a salad element. And it's not just the seeds that can be cooked—the leaves are a delicious, mildly bitter quick-cooking green.

1 1/3 cups (325 mL) amaranth

3 3/4 cups (925 mL) water

1 tsp (5 mL) cinnamon

1/2 tsp (2 mL) nutmeg

1/4 cup (60 mL) maple syrup, plus more for drizzling

zest from 1 lemon, finely grated

1 cup (250 mL) raspberries, or other fresh berries

Heat amaranth in a dry medium saucepan over medium-low, stirring constantly, until the grains start to pop, 1 to 2 minutes. Stir in water, increase heat to high and bring to a boil. Add cinnamon and nutmeg, stir again and reduce heat to low. Cover and cook for 25 minutes without stirring. Remove cover, add maple syrup and lemon zest and stir in the water that is left on top. Ladle into bowls and sprinkle raspberries on top. Serve with additional maple syrup on the side for drizzling.

1 serving: 295 Calories; 4.1 g Total Fat (0 g Mono, trace Poly, 13 g Sat); 0 mg Cholesterol; 57 g Carbohydrate (11.4 g Fibre, 13 g Sugar); 9 g Protein; 145 mg Sodium

Tip

Try substituting amaranth leaves for Swiss chard in our Stir-fried Swiss Chard (p. 48).

Amaranth seeds usually ripen and fall about the time of the first autumn frost. To harvest them, shake or rub the seedheads between your hands over a drop cloth, large bowl or bucket—wear gloves, because the seedheads can be quite coarse. The seeds and plant bits are easy to separate because the plant bits are lighter and rise to the surface if you run your hands through the collected seeds and carefully blow a fan over them. The seeds are quite light, too, so the breeze should not be too strong. Leave the seeds to dry in a warm place before storing them in an airtight container.

Artichoke and Fennel Strudels

Serves 8 to 10 as an appetizer

Artichokes are native to the Mediterranean. Those of us who grow them in Canada, so far away from their natural environment, do so out of love for this delectable thistle. Here, we pair slices of artichoke heart with licorice-flavoured fennel, rendered mellow and sweet with some cooking. Both vegetables are then cloaked in a blanket of puff pastry with creamy goat cheese. Because the filling can be made a day ahead and we use ready-to-bake puff pastry, this recipe is a great appetizer to make for your next dinner party (the filling can easily be doubled to serve more guests)—or serve it as a lunch with a salad of greens.

1 Tbsp (15 mL) grape seed oil

1/2 medium white onion, cut into 1/4-inch (0.6 cm) dice

1/2 bulb fennel, outer leaves removed, sliced thinly

1 medium-large artichoke

juice from 1 lemon

2 Tbsp (30 mL) sliced sun-dried tomatoes

1/2 cup (125 mL) water

sea salt and black pepper to taste

1 package of frozen puff pastry, thawed

2 oz (57 g) soft goat cheese

2 eggs, lightly beaten

Heat oil over medium-low in a medium saucepan, and add onion and fennel. Cook, stirring occasionally, until light golden brown, about 10 minutes.

Meanwhile, snap off the dark outer leaves of the artichoke, then slice off the cone. Cut or break off the stem, leaving just the bottom. Use a melon baller to scrape out the choke. Rub cut surfaces with lemon juice right away—artichokes oxidize very quickly. Slice thinly and coat with lemon juice again.

Add artichoke heart slices to the pan and cook, stirring occasionally, until they begin to colour, about 5 minutes. Increase heat to medium, add sun-dried tomatoes and water and cook, stirring occasionally, until the pan is almost dry and the artichoke hearts are tender. Remove from heat, season with salt and pepper, and set aside to cool completely. Can be done a day ahead up to this point.

Preheat oven to 400°F (200°C). Roll one sheet of puff pastry out into a 12 x 15 inch (30 x 38 cm) rectangle. With a sharp knife, cut into 10 rectangles, 6 x 3 inches (15 x 7.5 cm) each.

Place 2 Tbsp (30 mL) filling in the centre of every second rectangle. Top with a couple of dots of goat cheese. Brush the edges of each rectangle with beaten egg and top with a second rectangle of puff pastry. Crimp the edges with a fork. Transfer to a parchment-lined baking sheet. Repeat with the second sheet of puff pastry. Brush tops of strudels with beaten egg. Bake until puffed and golden, about 25 to 30 minutes.

1 strudel: 300 Calories; 20 g Total Fat (10 g Mono, 3.5 g Poly, 5 g Sat); trace Cholesterol; 24 g Carbohydrate (2 g Fibre, 1 g Sugar); 6 g Protein; 180 mg Sodium

Artichokes produce one large flower bud on the central stalk and many smaller flower buds on the side shoots. The flower buds are rounded and made up of tightly packed scales. They are usually ready for harvest as the scales just begin to loosen.

Baby Arugula with Basil Goat Cheese Wontons

Serves 4

Arugula is often mixed with other greens as a mesclun blend, but its mild, peppery bite is so versatile that you should consider planting a row or two of it. Replace lettuce with arugula to add flavour to sandwiches and burgers, and blend it into a pesto to sauce pasta or meat dishes with or to fold into egg dishes. Young leaves make a delicious salad without any other greens added; later, mix larger, more strongly flavoured arugula with other greens.

vegetable oil for deep frying

1/4 cup (60 mL) goat cheese

2 Tbsp (30 mL) fresh basil chiffonade (see Tip)

12 x 4 inch (10 cm) purchased wonton wrappers

4 cups (1 L) lightly packed baby arugula leaves

4 marinated artichoke hearts, thinly sliced

Sun-dried Tomato Vinaigrette (see opposite)

Combine goat cheese and basil in a small bowl and mix thoroughly. Lay wonton wrappers on a work surface. Drop a rounded teaspoon of goat cheese mixture in the centre of each one. Moisten the edges of the wrappers with water. Bring edges together, pushing out any air bubbles and pressing gently to seal—any trapped air will cause the wontons to burst when you fry them, expelling their contents. Wontons may be made up to 6 hours ahead up to this point. Store, covered and chilled, on a parchment-lined plate.

If you don't have a deep fryer, use a large saucepan to deep fry on your stove. Place at least 3 inches (7.5 cm) of vegetable oil in the saucepan, or follow manufacturer's directions for your deep fryer. Preheat the oil to 375°F (190°C).

Without crowding, drop wontons in batches into hot oil and fry until golden, 2 to 3 minutes. Remove from oil and drain on paper towels.

Toss arugula and artichokes with vinaigrette and divide among 4 plates. Arrange wontons on top and serve immediately.

1 serving: 530 Calories; 52 g Total Fat (37 g Mono, 8 g Poly, 7 g Sat); 10 mg Cholesterol; 17 g Carbohydrate (2 g Fibre, 6 g Sugar); 4 g Protein; 200 mg Sodium

Combine garlic, sun-dried tomatoes and vinegar in a small bowl. Use a hand blender to purée the tomatoes. Add basil. With the motor on, slowly drizzle in the oil and process until emulsified. Season with salt and pepper. Vinaigrette will keep, covered, in the refrigerator up to 4 days; blend again before using.

2 Tbsp (30 mL): 90 Calories; 10 g Total Fat (7 g Mono, 1 g Poly, 1.5 g Sat); 0 mg Cholesterol; 2 g Carbohydrates (0 g Fibre, trace Sugar); 0 g Protein; 10 mg Sodium

Tip

Chiffonade is a cutting technique in which a small stack of herb leaves are rolled tightly into a cigar shape and sliced thinly crosswise with a sharp knife; it produces long, thin slices of the herb, with less bruising.

Sun-dried Tomato Vinaigrette

1/2 clove garlic, minced

1/2 cup (125 mL) chopped and drained oil-packed sun-dried tomatoes

3 Tbsp (45 mL) balsamic vinegar

1/4 cup (60 mL) chopped fresh basil

1/2 cup (125 mL) olive oil

salt and black pepper to taste

Fettuccine with Asparagus, Prosciutto and Lemon Cream

Serves 4

Asparagus has almost become commonplace now that it is available year-round in grocery stores. But the sight of the first tender spears pushing their way through the earth in your own garden is sure to restore the sense of wonder due to what Louis XIV dubbed "the king of vegetables." This simple pasta dish screams spring: the vibrant green of the asparagus is complemented by a lively lemon flavour to wake up your taste buds from their winter slumber. It is a light and satisfying entrée on its own, or serve it as a side dish with grilled meat for a more substantial meal.

1/2 lb (225 g) prosciutto slices, cut crosswise into 1 inch (2.5 cm) wide pieces

1 bunch of asparagus, trimmed and cut into 2 inch (5 cm) sections

2 cups (500 mL) whipping cream

2 Tbsp (30 mL) finely grated lemon zest

2 Tbsp (30 mL) lemon juice

salt and black pepper to taste

1 lb (454 g) fresh fettuccine

1/4 cup (60 mL) grated Parmigiano-Reggiano

Heat a medium dry sauté pan over medium-high. Add prosciutto and cook, stirring occasionally, until crisp, about 5 minutes.

Bring a large saucepan of salted water to a boil. Add asparagus and cook for 1 to 2 minutes, depending on thickness (it should be slightly underdone, more crisp than tender); remove and refresh in ice water. Once chilled, transfer to a large colander placed in the sink.

Combine cream, lemon zest and juice in a medium saucepan. Bring to a boil over medium-high heat. Reduce heat to medium and cook until cream is reduced by about a third, about 5 minutes. Season with salt and pepper.

Meanwhile, add pasta to the same pot and the same water as asparagus and cook until al dente, about 5 minutes. Drain by pouring the water over the asparagus (to reheat it). Transfer pasta and asparagus to serving dish and toss with prosciutto and sauce. Sprinkle with cheese. Serve immediately.

1 serving: 560 Calories; 50 g Total Fat (12 g Mono, 1.5 g Poly, 28 g Sat); 190 mg Cholesterol; 50 g Carbohydrate (6 g Fibre, 6 g Sugar); 38 g Protein; 1190 mg Sodium

Tip

Thick or thin? The age-old debate rages on. To make the best of all the asparagus you grow, you should know the best ways to treat thick and thin spears. Thick stalks, though tender, tend to have tough skin; use a vegetable peeler to remove the skin below the top 3 to 4 inches (7.5 to 10 cm) and they'll cook perfectly. The thick, succulent stalks are ideal for grilling, steaming or poaching. Thin stalks, on the other hand, need no peeling and are perfect for stir-frying, roasting, or adding to pasta or rice dishes. Freeze the trimmings for Asparagus Bisque, p. 18.

Asparagus Bisque

Serves 6 to 8

If you plant your asparagus from seed, the two-year wait before you begin harvesting asparagus from your own patch may seem like 2000 years. But it will be well worth the wait—asparagus is at its best when it doesn't have to travel too far from field to plate—or bowl, in this case. Bisque was originally a creamy shellfish soup, but these days we make bisque from veggies too. It's a great way to use up those bits from the asparagus patch that may be oddly shaped or too short to use in dishes where their looks are more important.

2 lbs (900 g) asparagus pieces

2 Tbsp (30 mL) grape seed oil

2 medium white onions, chopped

1 leek, white and pale green parts only, washed well and chopped

6 cups (1.5 L) Vegetable Stock (see opposite)

bouquet garni (see p. 39)

1 cup (250 mL) whipping cream

Cut any tips off the stalks in 1 1/2 inch (4 cm) pieces and reserve. Chop remaining asparagus into 1 inch (2.5 cm) pieces. Set aside.

Heat oil in a large saucepan over medium-low. Add onions and leeks. Cook, stirring occasionally, until softened but not coloured, about 5 minutes. Add vegetable stock and *bouquet garni*. Bring to a simmer over medium-high heat. Reduce heat to medium. Simmer until leeks and onions are very soft, about 5 minutes. Add asparagus stalks. Simmer until asparagus is just tender, about 4 minutes. Remove and discard *bouquet garni*. Purée carefully in a blender (or with a hand blender). Pass through a fine-mesh sieve into a large bowl.

Transfer to cleaned saucepan and return to stove over medium-low. Stir in cream and heat just until hot.

Meanwhile, cut asparagus tips in half lengthwise. Blanch quickly in boiling water until just tender-crisp, 1 to 2 minutes depending on thickness.

Ladle bisque into individual bowls and garnish with asparagus tips. Bisque can be served hot or cold. If serving chilled, leave bisque in bowl after straining; set bowl immediately into a larger bowl partly filled with ice, stir in cream and serve.

1 serving: 200 Calories; 17 g Total Fat (4.5 g Mono, 4.5 g Poly, 7 g Sat); 40 mg Cholesterol; 11 g Carbohydrate (4 g Fibre, 4 g Sugar); 4 g Protein; 20 mg Sodium

Heat oil in a large saucepan over medium. Add onions and cook, stirring, until softened. Add remaining ingredients. Bring to a boil over medium-high heat. Reduce heat and cook just below a simmer for 40 minutes, stirring occasionally. Remove from heat. Strain through a colander and discard solids. Strain again through a cheesecloth-lined sieve and discard solids. Season lightly with salt. If not using immediately, cool, uncovered, to room temperature, then chill, covered. Keep covered in the refrigerator for up to 3 days, or freeze for up to 3 months.

1 cup (250 mL): 20 Calories; 2 g Total Fat (0 g Mono, 0 g Poly, 0 g Sat); 0 mg Cholesterol; 0 g Carbohydrate (0 g Fibre, 0 g Sugar); 0 g Protein; 0 mg Sodium

Tip

Using leftover, frozen asparagus trimmings will produce a less vibrant bisque, but the taste will be the same. Just substitute the stalks with more trimmings, cook and purée as directed.

Vegetable Stock

2 cups (500 mL) vegetable trimmings

4 tsp (20 mL) grape seed oil

2 medium yellow onions, chopped

4 stalks celery, chopped

2 medium carrots, chopped

1 bay leaf

1/4 cup (60 mL) coarsely chopped flat-leaf parsley

3 sprigs of fresh thyme

1/2 tsp (2 mL) whole black peppercorns

10 cups (2.5 L) water

salt to taste

Basil Aïoli Shrimp Rolls

Serves 4

One of my favourite things about gardening is having a variety of fresh herbs growing just steps from my kitchen. And one of my absolute favourite herbs is basil, in all its wonderful varieties, torn onto homemade pizza or tomato slices, shredded into a salad, mixed into a sauce or made into pesto. For about the same price as one of those little plastic packages you buy at the supermarket—which often contain not more than six leaves of basil—I can plant two whole rows of basil from seed in my garden. Not only does it help keep pests away from companion plants such as tomatoes, but it also perfumes the air with its distinctive spicy, licorice scent when I walk through the garden. Best of all, the more you pick, the better it grows. And once you see how versatile this basil aïoli is, you may want to plant an extra row of basil next year. In this recipe we've used the basil aïoli to dress shrimp for a twist on an East Coast lobster roll, but it could easily be served on the side with fresh veggies for dipping, spread onto a sandwich or pizza, dolloped on grilled fish or chicken or used anywhere instead of mayo—basil aïoli-dressed potato salad, anyone?

1 1/2 lbs (680 g) 21/30 size shrimp, shells on and deveined

4 1/2 tsp (22 mL) plus 1/4 cup (60 mL) coarse salt, *divided*

1 cup (250 mL) Basil Aïoli (see opposite)

4 top-loading hot dog buns or similar style

Combine shrimp with 4 1/2 tsp (22 mL) salt in a medium bowl. In a large bowl, prepare an ice water bath for the shrimp. Bring a large saucepan of water to a boil. Add 1/4 cup (60 mL) salt and return to a boil. Add shrimp and cook over medium-high heat until just cooked through, about 3 minutes. Drain immediately, then transfer to ice water bath until cool. Drain well. Remove and discard shells (or freeze to use for shellfish stock).

Place shrimp and aïoli in a medium bowl and toss to coat. Divide equally among buns and serve immediately. If you prefer a crunchier texture, toast the buns before filling with the shrimp mixture.

1 serving: 470 Calories; 24 g Total Fat (16 g Mono, 3.5 g Poly, 4 g Sat); 295 mg Cholesterol; 24 g Carbohydrate (1 g Fibre, 3 g Sugar); 39 g Protein; 820 mg Sodium

Combine egg yolk, garlic, salt and pepper in a food processor (or use a small bowl and a hand blender). Process until egg yolk lightens slightly in colour, about 1 minute. With the motor on, slowly drizzle in oil and process until emulsified. Add basil and process until incorporated. Transfer to a bowl and whisk in lemon juice. Aïoli can be prepared 1 day ahead and kept, covered, in the refrigerator.

1/4 cup (60 mL): 170 Calories; 19 g Total Fat (15 g Mono, 1.5 g Poly, 3 g Sat); 35 mg Cholesterol; trace Carbohydrate (0 g Fibre, 0 g Sugar); trace Protein; 100 mg Sodium

Basil Aïoli

1 egg yolk

2 cloves garlic, minced

1/4 tsp (1 mL) salt

pinch of black pepper

1/2 cup (125 mL) extra virgin olive oil

1/2 cup (125 mL) finely chopped fresh basil

1 Tbsp (15 mL) lemon juice

Seared Tuna Salade Niçoise

Serves 4

Salade Niçoise, whether the classic version with flaked, well-done tuna, or our modern take with slices of just-seared tuna, depends on very fresh beans for a large part of its appeal. It's even better when the beans are young and small—smaller than you'd likely find even at a farmers' market.

2 1/2 Tbsp (37 mL) minced shallot

2 Tbsp (30 mL) cider vinegar

2 Tbsp (30 mL) lemon juice

2 tsp (10 mL) Dijon mustard

1 clove garlic, minced and mashed to a paste

1 anchovy fillet or 1 tsp (5 mL) anchovy paste

1/2 cup (125 mL) extra virgin olive oil

1 1/2 tsp (7 mL) minced fresh thyme

3 1/2 Tbsp (52 mL) finely chopped fresh basil, *divided*

salt and black pepper to taste

3/4 lb (340 g) young green beans, trimmed

1 lb (454 g) small (1 to 2 inch, 2.5 to 5 cm) waxy potatoes

1 lb (454 g) 1 inch (2.5 cm) thick tuna steaks

grape seed oil for brushing

2 heads of Boston lettuce, leaves separated and large ones torn into pieces

(see next page)

For the dressing, combine shallots, vinegar, lemon juice, mustard, garlic paste and anchovy in a food processor (or use a hand blender and a small bowl) and process until well combined. With the motor on, slowly drizzle in oil and process until emulsified. Add thyme, 1 1/2 Tbsp (22 mL) basil, salt and pepper. Set aside.

In a large bowl, prepare an ice water bath. Boil a large saucepan of salted water. Add beans and cook just until crisp-tender, 2 to 4 minutes. With a slotted spoon, transfer to ice water. Once chilled, drain and set aside at room temperature.

Meanwhile, add potatoes to saucepan, return to a boil and simmer, uncovered, until tender, about 15 minutes. Drain and let cool enough to handle. Slice potatoes about 1/2 inch (12 mm) thick. Transfer to a medium bowl. Add 2 Tbsp (30 mL) dressing, toss to coat and set aside to cool to room temperature.

Preheat a dry sauté pan or lightly oiled grill pan over high. Lightly oil the tuna on all sides, then sprinkle with salt and pepper. Quickly sear tuna on all sides, about 2 minutes in

total, then transfer to a work surface to cool for 5 minutes. Slice tuna thinly across the grain.

In a large bowl, toss lettuce with about 2 Tbsp (30 mL) dressing. Divide among 4 plates. Divide beans into 4 equal portions and arrange on top. Repeat with potatoes, tomatoes, quartered eggs and olives. Divide tuna slices into 4 equal portions and add to the centre of each plate. Drizzle half of remaining dressing over top and sprinkle with capers, then parsley and 2 Tbsp (30 mL) basil. Serve immediately with remaining dressing on the side.

1 serving: 460 Calories; 16 g Total Fat (7 g Mono, 3 g Poly, 3.5 g Sat); 225 mg Cholesterol; 40 g Carbohydrate (9 g Fibre, 6 g Sugar); 40 g Protein; 880 mg Sodium

1 1/2 cups (375 mL) cherry or grape tomatoes, halved if large

4 hard-boiled eggs, peeled and quartered

1/2 cup (125 mL) Niçoise or other small brine-cured black olives

1/4 cup (60 mL) capers, drained and rinsed

2 Tbsp (30 mL) finely chopped fresh parsley

Ginger Pickled Green Beans

Makes about 8 cups (2 L)

Once you begin harvesting your beans, it seems like the harvest will never end—you need to be out in the garden picking beans every second day to avoid having them turn tough and stringy. But even if you can keep up with the harvest, you might not be able to keep up with the eating. Sure, you could lightly blanch them in boiling salted water, refresh quickly in ice water and freeze for a mid-winter taste of garden goodness. But what to do when you've got more beans than you know what to do with even after that? Pickle them!

2 lbs (900 g) green beans, trimmed

2 x 2 inch (5 cm) pieces of ginger, unpeeled

8 whole cloves garlic

4 small whole dried chilies

4 1/2 cups (1.25 L) unseasoned rice vinegar

2 1/2 cups (625 mL) water

1/4 cup (60 mL) soy sauce

1 Tbsp (15 mL) wasabi powder

Prepare an ice water bath. Bring a large saucepan of salted water to a boil. Working in 2 batches, add beans and cook 1 minute each, then transfer to ice water to cool. Once cool, drain well.

Place a metal rack in the bottom of a canner or very large saucepan. Add four 2 cup (500 mL) glass jars and water to fill, and surround the jars two thirds full. Cover and bring to a simmer over medium. Keep jars hot until ready to use. In a separate small saucepan, place lids and sealing rings in enough water to cover. Bring to a simmer over medium. Keep hot until ready to use.

Meanwhile, using a mandoline or vegetable peeler, slice ginger lengthwise as thinly as possible, discarding the outer pieces that are mostly peel. Drain jars and divide ginger among them. Add 2 cloves of garlic and 1 chili to each jar. Form beans into bundles in your hand, then stuff into jars. The tops of the beans must be at least 1 inch (2.5 cm) below the top of the jar; trim to fit if necessary.

Combine rice vinegar, water, soy sauce and wasabi in a large saucepan. Bring to a boil, then pour over beans in jars. The vinegar mixture should cover the beans by at least 1/2 inch (12 mm), and you should have another 1/2 inch (12 mm) head space in each jar. If the vinegar mixture does not come up high enough, heat a little more vinegar and water to add to the jars (at least 2 parts vinegar to 1 part water). Slide a non-metallic utensil such as a chopstick or small spatula down between the food and the jar in several places to release any air bubbles that might be trapped.

Fasten the lids to the jars according to the manufacturer's instructions. Place jars into water in canner and add more hot water to cover jars by 1 inch (2.5 cm). Cover canner and bring to a boil over high. Once water boils, process 10 minutes. Turn heat off and remove lid from canner. Let stand 5 minutes before carefully removing jars from the canner without tilting. Transfer to a kitchen towel on a work surface in a draft-free area to cool undisturbed for 24 hours.

Check each jar carefully to make sure it has sealed properly: the lid will appear concave. Jars that have not sealed properly should be transferred to the refrigerator and the contents eaten within 1 month. Remove screw-top rings. Store jars at room temperature at least 4 weeks, and up to 1 year, before eating.

1 cup (250 mL): 130 Calories; 0 g Total Fat (0 g Mono, 0 g Poly, 0 g Sat); 0 mg Cholesterol; 28 g Carbohydrate (4 g Fibre, 20 g Sugar); 3 g Protein; 45 mg Sodium

Fava Bean Risotto with Morels and Pea Vines

Serves 4

Fava beans, known in Italy as *carne di poveri* or "poor man's meat" because of their high protein content, and elsewhere in the world as broad beans, are one of the first plants in the garden to bear fruit. Early in the season they are small and tender and need only to be shelled before being lightly cooked and eaten. Later in the season, the larger beans inside the pod develop a thicker skin; they need to be shelled and the individual beans peeled before cooking (see Tip), but their nutty, buttery flavour is well worth it.

4 cups (1 L) vegetable stock (p. 19) or chicken stock

2 Tbsp (30 mL) *each* olive oil and butter, divided

6 oz (170 g) fresh morel mushrooms, cleaned and sliced

1/2 lb (225 g) fava beans, shelled

1 small onion, finely chopped

1 clove garlic, minced

1 cup (250 mL) Arborio or Carnaroli rice

1/2 cup (125 mL) dry white wine

1 cup (250 mL) fresh pea vines, plus a few more for garnish

1/3 cup (75 mL) freshly grated Parmesan

salt and black pepper to taste

In a medium saucepan, bring stock nearly to a boil, then reduce heat to low to keep warm.

In a large sauté pan, melt 1 Tbsp (15 mL) olive oil and 1 Tbsp (15 mL) butter over medium-low heat. Add morels and cook until tender, 3 to 5 minutes. Add favas and cook until warmed through, another 1 to 2 minutes. Season with salt and pepper and set aside.

In a large, heavy-bottomed saucepan, melt remaining olive oil and butter over medium-low heat. Add onion and cook until softened, about 3 minutes. Add garlic and cook another minute more. Add rice and cook, stirring constantly, until the grains of rice are mostly translucent but have an opaque centre, about 3 minutes. Add wine, stirring until the wine is almost completely absorbed. Add a ladleful of stock, about 1/2 to 3/4 cup (125 to 175 mL), and stir until almost completely absorbed. Continue adding stock one ladleful at a time and cooking, stirring constantly, until it is absorbed before adding another ladle of stock. After about 15 minutes, begin tasting the risotto before adding each new ladle of stock. When the rice is nearly done, firm but not crunchy, add another ladleful of stock, along with the favas, morels and pea vines. Continue stirring, and when the stock has been absorbed, the rice should be al dente. Stir in a little more stock along with the Parmesan, then season with salt and pepper. Serve immediately, topped with a few tender pea vine tips.

1 serving: 510 Calories; 16 g Total Fat (7 g Mono, 1.5 g Poly, 6 g Sat); 25 mg Cholesterol; 63 g Carbohydrate (16 g Fibre, 5 g Sugar); 23 g Protein; 740 mg Sodium

Tip

To shell favas, open the whole bean pod along the seam and pull each bean from the pod. Blanch the beans in salted water for 1 minute, then drain and chill in an ice water bath. Use your fingernails to pinch a bit of skin off one side of the bean. Squeeze the skin at the opposite side to pop the bean out.

Halibut with Hot and Sour Beet Relish

Serves 4

Would a beet grown anywhere else taste as sweet? The Canadian climate is perfect for beets. They grow well in most places throughout the summer, and a few early (or late) frosts only increase their sweetness. Nonetheless, many of us grow up eating beets only one way: pickled. So the true flavour of a beet, whether fresh, simmered or roasted, may come as a surprise the first time you taste it. The bright variety of colours from heirloom varieties, with their subtle variations in flavour—some sweeter, some earthier—is irresistible. Here the beets are lightly pickled in lime juice, but only very briefly. Their true flavour shines through and marries well with the mild halibut.

juice from 1 lime

2 Tbsp (30 mL) rice vinegar

2 inch (5 cm) piece of ginger, minced

1 1/2 tsp (7 mL) sriracha (Thai hot chili paste) or to taste

1 tsp (5 mL) sugar

1 cup (250 mL) grated beets

4 x 6 oz (170 g) halibut steaks, about 1 inch (2.5 cm) thick

1 Tbsp (15 mL) grape seed oil

salt and black pepper to taste

Whisk together lime juice, rice vinegar, ginger, sriracha, sugar and salt in a medium bowl. (Divide marinade among several bowls if using several types of beets.) Add grated beets and toss to coat. Cover and refrigerate 1 hour.

Heat a dry sauté pan over medium-high. Lightly oil halibut on both sides, then sprinkle with salt and pepper. Add halibut to hot pan and cook 6 minutes before turning. Cook on second side until just cooked through, 3 to 4 minutes more. Transfer to serving plates. Divide beets into 4 equal portions and pile on top of halibut. Serve immediately.

1 serving: 280 Calories; 8 g Total Fat (2.5 g Mono, 4 g Poly, 1 g Sat); 65 mg Cholesterol; 6 g Carbohydrate (1 g Fibre, 5 g Sugar); 47 g Protein; 180 mg Sodium

Tip

You can use any variety of beets for this recipe, or use several, as we did—just be sure to marinate each colour in a separate container and combine them only at the last minute.

Beets mature in 45 to 80 days, depending on the variety. Short-season beets are best for immediate eating and preserving, and long-season beets are the better choice for storing. Pick beets as soon as they are big enough to eat. They are tender when young but can become woody as they mature.

Lemon Shortbread-topped Blackberry Cobbler

Serves 4

No matter whether your blackberry gardening involves encouraging it to grow or trying to discourage it from taking over your garden, blackberries are always delicious, with their distinctive earthy, winey flavour. Use your harvest to make this classic blackberry cobbler with a unique lemon shortbread topping. Leftover shortbread dough can be re-rolled and made into cookies. Just bake them afterwards in a 375°F (190°C) oven for 10 to 15 minutes.

1/2 lb (225 g) butter

1/2 cup (125 mL) confectioner's sugar

1 egg, lightly beaten

1/2 tsp (2 mL) vanilla extract

zest from 1 lemon

1 cup (250 mL) all-purpose flour

1 cup (250 mL) rice flour

1/2 tsp (2 mL) baking powder

1/4 tsp (1 mL) sea salt

6 cups (1.5 L) fresh blackberries

1/2 cup (125 mL) granulated sugar

2 Tbsp (30 mL) cornstarch

3/4 tsp (4 mL) ground allspice

1 Tbsp (15 mL) butter

In the bowl of a mixer fitted with the paddle attachment, cream butter until fluffy. Add sugar slowly and beat until incorporated. Beat in egg, then add vanilla and lemon zest and mix well.

In a medium bowl, sift together the two flours, baking powder and salt. Add half this mixture to the mixer and beat until incorporated. Add remaining flour mixture and beat until just combined. Form dough into a disc, wrap with plastic and chill for about 30 minutes.

For the filling, preheat oven to 375°F (190°C). Butter the bottoms and sides of 4 teacups or 1 cup (250 mL) soufflé dishes.

Taste the berries to judge how sweet they are. If they are very sweet, you'll want to use less sugar; if they are very tart, you'll want to use more. In a large mixing bowl, blend sugar, cornstarch and allspice. Add the blackberries and toss gently. Distribute the berries evenly among the dishes (they should be heaped in the cups) and dot with butter. Bake until the berry mixture begins to bubble, about 15 minutes. Remove from oven.

On a lightly floured cutting board, roll out the dough to about 1/2 inch (12 mm) thick. Use a fifth teacup or cookie cutter to cut circles to fit the cups. Cut a slit in the middle to let the steam escape. Place the dough over the hot berries in each cup. Return to the oven and bake until the shortbread turns a pale golden colour, 15 to 20 minutes. Remove from the oven and let cool 10 minutes before serving.

1 serving: 470 Calories; 20 g Total Fat (5 g Mono, 1.5 g Poly, 12 g Sat); 65 mg Cholesterol; 72 g Carbohydrates (12 g Fibre, 39 g Sugar); 5 Protein; 200 mg Sodium

Tip

The rice flour helps give this shortbread topping its light texture, but if you don't have rice flour, add another cup (250 mL) of all-purpose flour.

Salmon with Blueberry Lavender Reduction

Serves 4

Blueberries are one of the few plants in our edible garden that are native to Canada, so they're a snap to grow. And they're so delicious eaten out of hand that we don't need to think much beyond cooking them into pancakes and pies, or perhaps adding them to a salad. But blueberries are delicious in dishes beyond salads. In this recipe we've turned them into a sauce for another Canadian native, salmon, but the sauce would be just as delicious on chicken, pork or another fish. Steamed green beans lightly dressed with Lemon Oil make the perfect match for this dish.

grape seed oil, as needed

1 cup (250 mL) fresh blueberries, and a few more for garnish

1 cup (250 mL) champagne vinegar

3/4 cup (175 mL) granulated sugar

1/2 tsp (2 mL) dried lavender, and a few sprigs for garnish

1/4 tsp (1 mL) salt

4 x 6 oz (170 g) salmon fillets

salt and black pepper to taste

Preheat grill to medium-high. Clean thoroughly with a wire brush. Use a rag to rub a little grape seed oil on the grill.

Combine blueberries, champagne vinegar, sugar, lavender and salt in a small saucepan. Bring to a low simmer and cook until the mixture is reduced by about half and coats the back of a spoon. Use a wooden spoon to press the sauce through a fine-mesh sieve.

While the sauce is reducing, cook the fish. Season the fillets with salt and pepper. Place on the grill skin side up. Cook until the thinnest edge becomes opaque, 3 to 5 minutes, depending on thickness. Slip a long spatula under the fillet from the side, lifting the entire fillet at once, to flip. If the fillet sticks at all, leave it for another 30 seconds before trying again. Cook on the second side only to brown the outside, about 2 minutes more.

To serve, place fillets on a plate and spoon sauce around fillets and over top. Garnish with a few fresh blueberries and a sprig of lavender.

1 serving: 470 Calories; 16 g Total Fat (4.5 g Mono, 8 g Poly, 2 g Sat); 110 mg Cholesterol; 41 g Carbohydrate (trace Fibre, 40 g Sugar); 40 g Protein; 250 mg Sodium

Check lemon zest strips for any pith and slice it off with a small, sharp knife. Heat oil in a small saucepan over medium-low. Add zest and simmer about 5 minutes. Turn off heat and let stand, uncovered, about 30 minutes before straining through a fine-mesh sieve. Keeps, covered and chilled, for up to 2 weeks—once you try it, you'll find a multitude of ways to use it up. If you have lemon-scented herbs in your garden, you could substitute 1/3 cup (75 mL) coarsely chopped lemon verbena, lemon balm or lemon-scented geranium for the lemon zest.

2 Tbsp (30 mL): 240 Calories; 28 g Total Fat (6 g Mono, 20 g Poly, 2 g Sat); 0 mg Cholesterol; 0 g Carbohydrate (0 g Fibre, 0 g Sugar); 0 g Protein; 0 mg Sodium

Lemon Oil

1/2 cup (125 mL) grape seed oil

zest from 2 lemons, cut off in strips with a peeler rather than zested

Broccoli and Pesto Pizza on the Grill

Serves 4

If you haven't yet tried broccoli on your pizza, run, don't walk, to get started on this recipe. The broccoli caramelizes along with the cheese, bringing out sweetness that you never knew was there.

flour for dusting

premade dough for 2 x 12 inch (30 cm) pizza crusts

1/2 cup (125 mL) basil pesto

1 1/2 cups (375 mL) broccoli florets, blanched and refreshed

1 cup (250 mL) thinly sliced mushrooms, sautéed until tender

medium red onion, thinly sliced

1 1/2 cups (375 mL) grated jalapeño Jack cheese

Dust work surface lightly with flour. With floured hands, transfer the 2 dough balls to the work surface. Sprinkle with flour, then flatten each one into a 5 inch (12 cm) wide disc. Sprinkle with flour again, wrap with plastic wrap and let rest at room temperature for 2 hours.

Preheat grill to high (see Tip, below). Dust the outside bottom of a baking pan with cornmeal. With a floured rolling pin, roll one disc out to 12 inches (30 cm). Lay the dough on the outside bottom of the pan to transfer to the grill. Slip off the pan directly onto the grill rack. Close lid and cook for 3 to 4 minutes, just until set, but not coloured. Meanwhile, roll out the second ball of dough as above. Transfer second crust to grill and transfer first to work surface.

Tip

This pizza could also be cooked in a regular oven. Preheat the oven as high as it will go, add all your toppings to uncooked dough, then bake about 8 minutes on a preheated pizza stone or cold baking sheet.

Flip crust so that the side that was directly over the heat faces up. Spread 1/4 cup (60 mL) pesto over top, leaving a little crust uncovered around the edges. Sprinkle with 3/4 cup (175 mL) broccoli florets, 1/2 cup (125 mL) mushrooms and half the sliced onion. Top with 3/4 cup (175 mL) cheese. Return to grill to cook with lid closed for 3 to 4 minutes, until the cheese is melted and bubbling and the exposed crust is golden. Transfer to work surface and let rest about 3 minutes before cutting and serving. Repeat with second pizza crust.

1 serving: 530 Calories; 33 g Total Fat (3.5 g Mono, 0.5 g Poly, 11 g Sat); 35 mg Cholesterol; 41 g Carbohydrate (3 g Fibre, 4 g Sugar); 20 g Protein; 860 mg Sodium

Pan-roasted Brussels Sprouts Pasta

Serves 4

Chances are if you've got Brussels sprouts growing in your garden, you're already a fan. And you've probably moved beyond boiling or steaming and have been won over by the play of contrasting flavours and textures of roasted Brussels sprouts. They are one of the few veggies that you almost always see cooked on its own, or with a few accents such as bacon or nuts; we rarely think to include Brussels sprouts as an element of another dish, the way we would broccoli or tomatoes. Here we pan-roast sliced sprouts until golden and crisp on the outside and tender on the inside, then add them to pasta for a tasty and comforting, yet simple, dish.

2 cups (500 mL) medium-sized pasta shapes, such as rotini or shells

24 small Brussels sprouts

2 Tbsp (30 mL) grape seed oil

salt and black pepper to taste

2 Tbsp (30 mL) extra virgin olive oil

1/4 cup (60 mL) capers, drained and rinsed

1/4 cup (60 mL) finely grated Parmesan

zest and juice from 1 lemon

Bring a large saucepan of salted water to a boil. Add pasta and cook, stirring occasionally just until al dente, 8 to 10 minutes. Drain and return to saucepan.

Meanwhile, trim the stem ends of the Brussels sprouts; pull off and discard any ragged outer leaves. Slice each sprout vertically into 3 or 4 pieces about 1/2 inch (12 mm) thick. Transfer to a large bowl, add grape seed oil and a pinch of salt and pepper. Toss to coat. Heat a large sauté pan over medium-high. Add sprouts in a single layer and cook until golden brown, 3 to 4 minutes. Flip them over and cook until golden brown on the second side and tender all the way through, another 3 to 4 minutes. Add to pasta in saucepan. Drizzle olive oil over top, and add capers, Parmesan and lemon zest and juice. Toss to coat and serve immediately.

1 serving: 330 Calories; 17 g Total Fat (5 g Mono, 6 g Poly, 3 g Sat); 5 mg Cholesterol; 46 g Carbohydrate (7 g Fibre, 4 g Sugar); 12 g Protein; 360 mg Sodium

You'll get the best flavour if you pick your sprouts when they are small with tightly closed heads. A light frost can improve the flavour of the sprouts. The entire plant can be pulled up, and if you remove the roots, leaves and top of the plant, the sprouts can be stored on the stem in a cool place for up to four weeks. Be sure to keep an eye on them because they can go bad quickly. They can also be frozen for later use.

Cabbage Roll Soup

Serves 4 to 8

For many Canadians, cabbage is made and grown for cabbage rolls. It's true that cabbage rolls are one of the most perfect forms of comfort food—warm, hearty, filling and homey. The only trouble is that making them can take a long time. We've turned them into a soup that has all the familiar flavours and is just as hearty, but is quick and easy to boot.

1 lb (454 g) lean ground beef

4 oz (113 g) smoked kielbasa sausage, sliced

1 medium onion, cut into 1/2 inch (12 mm) dice

2 cloves garlic, minced

1 Tbsp (15 mL) paprika

6 cups (1.5 L) beef broth

1 × 5 1/2 oz (156 mL) can of tomato paste

3/4 cup (175 mL) long grain rice

2 tsp (2 mL) salt

1 tsp (5 mL) black pepper

bouquet garni (see opposite)

1/2 head Savoy cabbage, sliced 1/2 inch (12 mm) wide

Place ground beef in a large saucepan. Cook, stirring, over medium heat until browned and just cooked through, 3 to 4 minutes. Add sausage, onion, garlic and paprika, and cook until sausage is cooked through and onions have softened, about 5 minutes more. Stir in broth, tomato paste, rice, salt and pepper. Bring to a boil. Stir, add *bouquet garni,* cover and reduce heat to medium-low. Simmer about 10 minutes, add sliced cabbage and simmer another 15 minutes, until cabbage is tender and rice is cooked. Remove and discard bouquet garni and serve soup immediately, with sour cream on the side if desired.

1 serving: 350 Calories; 12 g Total Fat (4.5 g Mono, 0 g Poly, 4 g Sat); 60 mg Cholesterol; 30 g Carbohydrate (3 g Fibre, 6 g Sugar); 24 g Protein; 1210 mg Sodium

Tip

A *bouquet garni* is a small bundle of herbs used to flavour stocks and soups. The ingredients vary depending on the dish, but the basic version is a sprig each of parsley and thyme and one bay leaf, all tied together or placed in a bag of cheesecloth for easy removal before serving.

When a good-sized head of cabbage has developed, cut it cleanly from the plant. Smaller heads often develop once the main head has been cut. Plants are frost hardy, and the last of the cabbages can be left in the ground through autumn, then stored in a cold, frost-free location.

Chilled Carrot Citrus Soup with Mint

Serves 4

Toward the end of spring, days get longer and finally start to heat up; backyards begin to fill in with new green growth to cover up the brown earth; and we start to reap the first rewards of our efforts in the garden. Smaller and less sweet than later in the year, early carrots are still irresistible pulled fresh from the ground, the dirt wiped off on your shirt and eaten while you're still standing in the garden. If you can suppress that urge long enough to make a decent harvest, this soup pairs those early carrots with citrus and mint for a bright refreshing starter.

3 Tbsp (45 mL) grape seed oil

1 medium onion, finely chopped

4 cups (1 L) thinly sliced carrots

1/4 tsp (1 mL) *each* salt and black pepper

generous pinch *each* ground cloves and coriander

4 cups (1 L) water

1 cup (250 mL) freshly squeezed orange juice

2 tsp (10 mL) fresh lemon juice

3 Tbsp (45 mL) chopped fresh mint

sprigs of mint for garnish

Heat oil in a large saucepan over medium-low. Add onion and cook, stirring, until golden, about 5 minutes. Add carrots, salt, pepper, cloves and coriander. Cook, stirring, about 5 minutes; add water and bring to a boil. Reduce heat, cover and simmer until carrots are very tender, about 15 minutes. Purée soup with a hand blender (or in a blender, see Tip) until very smooth, about 1 minute. Transfer to a large bowl. Stir in orange and lemon juices and chopped mint. Cover and chill until cold, at least 2 hours. Serve garnished with sprigs of mint.

1 serving: 180 Calories; 11 g Total Fat (2.5 g Mono, 8 g Poly, 1 g Sat); 0 mg Cholesterol; 22 g Carbohydrate (4 g Fibre, 7 g Sugar); 2 g Protein; 240 mg Sodium

Tip

Work carefully when you purée hot liquids in a blender. Process in several small batches instead of one large amount.

Never judge carrots by their greens. Big, bushy tops are no indication that carrots are ready for picking. As the roots develop, you will often see the top of the carrots at or just above soil level—a better indication of their development.

Steamed Carrots with Mint

Serves 4

Multicoloured carrots are starting to appear everywhere, from backyard gardens to mainstream grocers, but people who grow them know they're not really the novelty that many think they are. Carrots originally came in a variety of colours, most often red, white or black. Our familiar orange carrots are the result of selective breeding with a mutant yellow carrot. The purple, red, yellow and black varieties are mainly heirloom varieties that have been cultivated for more than 100 years in various parts of the world. Steamed with mint and tossed with honey, these carrots are infused with a mild flavour that takes them beyond ordinary. For variety, try substituting a different herb, such as tarragon, lemon verbena or dill, for the mint.

4 large fresh sprigs of mint

1 lb (454 g) carrots with some of their green tops attached, peeled or scrubbed (see Tip)

1 1/2 Tbsp (22 mL) butter at room temperature

2 tsp (10 mL) honey

1 Tbsp (15 mL) chopped fresh mint

coarse salt and black pepper to taste

Place mint sprigs in the bottom of a large saucepan. Place a steamer rack in the pan. Add enough water to touch the bottom of the steamer rack. Arrange carrots on the rack. Cover and set over high heat to steam until carrots are just tender, 8 to 10 minutes. Transfer carrots to a medium bowl; toss with butter, honey and chopped mint. Sprinkle with salt and pepper and serve.

1 serving: 90 Calories; 4.5 g Total Fat (1 g Mono, 0 g Poly, 3 g Sat); 10 mg Cholesterol; 13 g Carbohydrate (2 g Fibre, 8 g Sugar); trace Protein; 120 mg Sodium

Tip

For some of the coloured carrots, beauty really is only skin deep. Many of the purple and red varieties have brightly coloured skins with yellow or orange interiors. To make the most of them, scrub lightly to remove all the dirt, rather than peeling them. The very dark varieties, on the other hand, are so full of colour that when cooked with other vegetables (or other colours of carrot), they'll turn everything a murky colour. These carrots are best cooked on their own and mixed with others at the last minute.

Red Curry Cauliflower

Serves 4

Cauliflower is another oft-maligned member of the cabbage family. Some people complain that it's bland, some that it's too cabbagey. The truth is, cauliflower is a bit of a chameleon. Raw, it does have a bit of a cabbagey bite, making it a perfect carrier for dips; steamed or simmered until fully tender, it becomes smooth and creamy and can be puréed into a velvety-smooth soup or sauce; roasted until golden, it becomes crisp on the outside, tender on the inside and nutty-flavoured. Cauliflower also has a remarkable capacity to absorb other flavours through and through, which is one of the reasons that it's so good in a curry.

1 Tbsp (15 mL) grape seed oil

1/2 medium onion, cut into 1/2 inch (12 mm) dice

1/3 cup (75 mL) Red Curry Paste (see opposite) or to taste

1 × 14 oz (398 mL) can of coconut milk

2 small or 1 large head of cauliflower, cut into florets

1/2 cup (125 mL) thinly sliced green onion

1/4 cup (60 mL) chopped fresh cilantro

1/4 cup (60 mL) chopped peanuts

Heat oil in a large saucepan over medium. Add onion and cook, stirring, until light golden. Add curry paste and cook, stirring, another 1 to 2 minutes. Add coconut milk and bring to a boil. Add cauliflower and return to a boil. Reduce heat to medium-low, cover and simmer until cauliflower is tender, about 15 minutes. Stir in green onions. Transfer to serving dish and sprinkle with cilantro and peanuts. Serve immediately over jasmine rice.

1 serving: Calories; 32 g Total Fat (4.5 g Mono, 6 g Poly, 20 g Sat); trace Cholesterol; 22 g Carbohydrate (5 g Fibre, 7 g Sugar); 10 g Protein; 75 mg Sodium

Put all ingredients except the oil into a blender and purée to a smooth paste, adding only as much of the oil as necessary to get the blender moving. Transfer to a clean jar, cover with a layer of grape seed oil, and keep refrigerated up to 1 week.

1/3 cup (75 mL): 200 Calories; 11 g Total Fat (2.5 g Mono, 7 g Poly, 1 g Sat); 15 mg Cholesterol; 22 g Carbohydrate (4 g Fibre, 8 g Sugar); 6 g Protein; 30 mg Sodium

When seed shopping, watch for the various brightly coloured varieties of cauliflower, as well as the beautiful heirloom chartreuse Romanesco variety, pictured here, which looks like a whimsical space-age fairy castle. It's sometimes sold as a broccoli variety or as "broccoflower," perhaps because of its green hue, but in taste and texture is much more cauliflower than broccoli.

Red Curry Paste

10 hot red chilies

3 lemongrass stalks, thinly sliced

4 inch (10 cm) piece of galangal (or fresh ginger), finely grated

2 Tbsp (30 mL) chopped cilantro root

2 Tbsp (30 mL) chopped fresh cilantro

5 cloves garlic, minced

4 tsp (20 mL) shrimp paste

2 tsp (10 mL) cumin seeds

2 tsp (10 mL) coriander seeds

2 tsp (10 mL) peppercorns

2 Tbsp (30 mL) grape seed oil

Celery and Apple Salad

Serves 4

Celery's bright chartreuse colour and bushy leaves make it a great addition not just to the kitchen garden, but to the flower garden as well. In the kitchen, however, it is often underappreciated, used to add crunch to dishes such as traditional stuffing, or as nothing more than a carrier for that ubiquitous orange cheese-flavoured spread. But it is one of the cornerstones of traditional French cuisine, one of the holy trinity of vegetables that form *mirepoix,* the flavour base of almost every stock, soup and sauce. Here celery regains its elegance, shaved into thin wisps and tossed with apple and celery-flavoured croutons in a honey lime dressing.

2/3 cup (150 mL) firm white bread cubes, cut into 1/2 inch (12 mm) dice

1/4 cup (60 mL) grape seed oil

1/4 tsp (1 mL) celery salt

4 celery ribs, with leaves

Honey Lime Dressing (see opposite)

2 Tbsp (30 mL) lime juice

cold water, as needed

2 large sweet apples, such as gala

2 Tbsp (30 mL) finely chopped fresh chives

Preheat oven to 400°F (200°C). Place bread in a medium bowl, drizzle oil over and toss to coat. Spread in a single layer on a baking sheet and sprinkle with celery salt. Cook, stirring occasionally, until golden brown all over, about 10 minutes. Set aside to cool to room temperature.

Peel outer strings from celery ribs, then cut into 2 inch (5 cm) lengths. Use a mandoline (or cut by hand) to julienne. Add to dressing in bowl. Place lime juice in a medium bowl. Core apples and julienne. Add immediately to lime juice and toss well to coat. If any lime juice remains in the bowl, drain it off and discard. Add apple to celery. Add croutons and toss well. Divide among 4 serving plates and sprinkle with chives. Serve immediately.

Combine lime juice, mustard and honey in a large bowl. Stir well to combine. Drizzle in olive oil, stirring all the while. Add salt and pepper and adjust seasoning to taste.

1 serving: 310 Calories; 25 g Total Fat (11 g Mono, 11 g Poly, 2.5 g Sat); 0 mg Cholesterol; 25 g Carbohydrate (3 g Fibre, 14 g Sugar); 2 g Protein; 210 mg Sodium

Honey Lime Dressing

1 Tbsp (15 mL) fresh lime juice

1/2 tsp (7 mL) grainy mustard

1/4 tsp (6 mL) honey

3 Tbsp (45 mL) extra virgin olive oil

salt and black pepper to taste

Stir-fried Swiss Chard

Serves 4

One of the real treats of growing your own produce is the flavour of truly fresh vegetables. Swiss chard is one whose flavour can change not over days, but within hours. Not to say that you can't get delicious chard from the farmers' market—you can, and it's certain to taste much better than what you'll find at the grocery store. But straight from the garden it will be crisper and sweeter, and only mildly bitter. At planting time, watch for seed packets labelled "Rainbow Chard"— they contain red-, pink-, orange-, yellow- and white-stemmed varieties that will bring a burst of colour to garden and plate.

1 Tbsp (15 mL) grape seed oil

3 cloves garlic, minced

2 Tbsp (30 mL) minced ginger

3 Tbsp (45 mL) rice vinegar

2 Tbsp (30 mL) soy sauce

2 tsp (10 mL) sugar

12 cups (3 L) Swiss chard, cut crosswise into 2 inch (5 cm) wide strips (see Tip)

1 Tbsp (15 mL) sesame oil

2 Tbsp (30 mL) sesame seeds

Heat oil in a wok over medium-high. Add garlic and cook, stirring constantly, until just starting to colour. Add ginger and cook, stirring constantly, until fragrant. Add rice vinegar, soy sauce and sugar and cook, stirring, just until sugar dissolves. Add Swiss chard and cook, stirring, just until wilted, 3 to 5 minutes. Add sesame oil and toss to coat. Sprinkle with sesame seeds and serve immediately.

1 serving: 130 Calories; 10 g Total Fat (3 g Mono, 5 g Poly, 1 g Sat); 0 mg Cholesterol; 10 g Carbohydrate (2 g Fibre, 5 g Sugar); 4 g Protein; 690 mg Sodium

Tip

If your chard leaves are large, the stalks and central ribs may be tough. Just cut the leaves off and slice stalks and leaves separately, then cook the stalks in the pan for about 2 minutes before adding the leaves.

Chard matures quickly, and a few leaves can be plucked from each plant every week or so all summer. You can generally start picking leaves about a month after the seed sprouts and continue to do so until the plant is killed back by frost.

Chive Ricotta Gnocchi

Serves 8

Chives are one of the herbs that almost everyone grows in their garden, and for good reason—they are one of the easiest herbs to grow. They'll adapt to almost any growing conditions, put up beautiful flowers in the spring (and if you're lucky, in the fall, too), and no matter what, they'll always be back after the winter. But don't take that as a reason to ignore them. A confetti-like sprinkle of tiny rounds of chopped chives will lend bright colour and a delicate onion flavour to almost any dish. Here we've incorporated them into the dough of a homemade ricotta gnocchi, which is quicker to make and much less prone to toughness than the potato variety. Then, rather than boiling the gnocchi in the more traditional way, we've pan-fried them for a crunchy, caramelized outside and a soft, fluffy inside, and of course we finish with an extra sprinkle of chives for good measure.

2 egg yolks

2 cups (500 mL) whole milk ricotta

1 1/4 cups (300 mL) freshly grated Parmesan, *divided*

1/2 cup (125 mL) plus 2 Tbsp (30 mL) finely chopped chives, *divided*

1 tsp (5 mL) lemon zest

2 tsp (10 mL) coarse salt

1 1/2 cups (375 mL) all-purpose flour, *divided*

2 Tbsp (30 mL) butter

1 Tbsp (15 mL) olive oil

Place egg yolks in a large bowl. Add ricotta and 1 cup (250 mL) Parmesan and mix well. Fold in 1/2 cup (125 mL) chives, lemon zest and salt. Sprinkle half the flour over top, and fold in until incorporated. Sprinkle remaining flour over top and knead gently with your hands to bring the dough together, 1 to 2 minutes. The dough should be smooth and soft. Divide the dough into 8 portions. Transfer 1 portion to a lightly floured work surface and roll into a 1 inch (2.5 cm) thick log. Cut into 3/4 inch (2 cm) pieces (see below). Transfer gnocchi to a lightly floured baking sheet and sprinkle a little flour over top so they don't stick together. Repeat with remaining logs. If you're cooking for just a few people, some of the gnocchi may be frozen on the baking sheet at this point. Transfer to a freezer bag or sealed container once fully frozen. Gnocchi will keep frozen up to 3 months.

Heat a sauté pan over medium-high. Add butter and olive oil. Once butter has lightly browned, add gnocchi in a single layer. Cook until golden brown, about 2 minutes. Turn over and cook on second side until golden and no longer tasting of flour, about 2 minutes more. Add remaining Parmesan and chives. Toss and serve immediately.

1 serving: 230 Calories; 12 g Total Fat (4 g Mono, 1 g Poly, 6 g Sat); 85 mg Cholesterol; 22 g Carbohydrate (trace Fibre, 3 g Sugar); 11 g Protein; 830 mg Sodium

Chives can be snipped off with scissors all spring, summer and autumn, as needed. The youngest leaves are the most tender and flavourful, so cut plants back to encourage new growth if flavour diminishes over summer.

Cilantro-stuffed Chicken Thighs

Serves 4

Cilantro seems to be an herb that people either love or hate. Not to say that no one can be converted—I was once a cilantro hater, but now I couldn't imagine eating some of my favourite dishes without it. The first time I grew cilantro in my garden at home, I was startled by how different it looked from the cilantro that you buy at grocery stores. Sure, there are some fat leaves down near the base, but the top half of the plant is delicate and feathery, and its white flowers are beautiful in the garden and tasty chopped into salads or other dishes that call for a mild dose of cilantro flavour. For this dish, we've blended cilantro into a flavourful paste that's stuffed under the skin of chicken thighs, with a little more drizzled over top.

4 cups (1 L) lightly packed cilantro leaves, plus more for garnish

1/2 cup (125 mL) macadamia nuts

2 Tbsp (30 mL) lime juice

2 Tbsp (30 mL) minced fresh ginger

1 Tbsp (15 mL) lime zest

1 Tbsp (15 mL) sriracha (Thai hot chili paste)

salt and black pepper to taste

1/4 cup (60 mL) plus 1 Tbsp (15 mL) grape seed oil, *divided*

8 chicken thighs

Combine cilantro, macadamia nuts, lime juice, ginger, lime zest and sriracha in a food processor or blender. Pulse until finely chopped, then with the motor on add 1/4 cup (60 mL) oil slowly to form a paste. Season with salt. Transfer about half to a small bowl and reserve the rest.

Preheat oven to 375°F (190°C). Use a finger to make a pocket between the skin and the meat of each chicken thigh. Place 1 rounded spoonful into each pocket, then press down on the skin to spread the paste through the whole pocket. (If you use up all the cilantro paste in your bowl, use a clean spoon to transfer some more into the bowl to avoid cross contamination.) Arrange thighs skin side up in a single layer on a wire rack set in a baking sheet. Brush the skin lightly with remaining oil and sprinkle with salt and pepper. Roast until cooked through, about 45 minutes (when pierced with a knife the juices should run clear). Transfer to a serving platter, drizzle remaining paste over top, and garnish with a few more cilantro leaves. Serve immediately.

1 serving: 480 Calories; 37 g Total Fat (16 g Mono, 14 g Poly, 4.5 g Sat); 140 mg Cholesterol; 5 g Carbohydrate (2 g Fibre, 2 g Sugar); 35 g Protein; 230 mg Sodium

The herb we call cilantro is actually the leaves of the coriander plant. The seeds of the plant, called coriander, are also edible, but the flavour of each is quite distinct, so coriander and cilantro are not interchangeable. The leaves can be harvested as needed throughout summer. Plant smaller sowings two weeks apart to ensure a steady supply of leaves.

Seared Scallops with Roasted Corn Relish and Sweet Corn Sauce

Serves 4 as an appetizer

Gardeners all seem to have sort of a love/hate relationship with summer. On the one hand, it means the end of the garden's glory days are near. On the other hand, it is when we start to reap much of the garden's bounty, with corn near the very top of the list. If you have so much corn that corn on the cob, picked minutes before it goes into the pot or onto the grill, starts to seem boring, then you'll want to try this recipe.

1 Tbsp (15 mL) grape seed oil

1 lb (454 g) jumbo scallops

salt and black pepper to taste

Heat oil in a sauté pan over medium-high. Sprinkle scallops on both sides with salt and pepper. Add to the pan and cook until golden, 2 to 3 minutes. Turn and cook on second side until golden brown and just cooked through, another 2 to 3 minutes, depending on their size.

Spoon an equal amount of corn sauce onto 4 plates. Divide scallops among the plates, placing them on top of the sauce. Pile relish on top and serve immediately.

1 serving: 250 Calories; 6 g Total Fat (1 g Mono, 3.5 g Poly, 0.5 g Sat); 35 mg Cholesterol; 29 g Carbohydrate (4 g Fibre, 6 g Sugar); 23 g Protein; 320 mg Sodium

Roasted Corn Relish

1 cup (250 mL) fresh corn kernels

1 small red chili pepper, finely chopped

zest and juice from 1 lime

1/4 tsp (1 mL) salt

1 large peach, cut into 1/2 inch (12 mm) dice

2 Tbsp (30 mL) chopped fresh cilantro

2 Tbsp (30 mL) fresh basil chiffonade (see Tip, p. 15)

Heat a dry medium sauté pan over medium-high. Add corn kernels and cook, stirring occasionally, until light golden brown, 3 to 4 minutes. Stir in chopped chili and cook another minute. Add lime zest, juice and salt. Transfer to a small bowl to cool slightly. Once cool, stir in peach, cilantro and basil.

1 serving: 50 Calories; 0.5 g Total Fat (0 g Mono, 0 g Poly, 0 g Sat); 0 mg Cholesterol; 11 g Carbohydrate (trace Fibre, 4 g Sugar); trace Protein; 125 mg Sodium

Sweet Corn Sauce

2 cups (500 mL) fresh corn kernels

1/2 cup (125 mL) water

1/4 tsp (1 mL) vanilla

1 Tbsp (15 mL) lime juice

salt and black pepper to taste

Combine corn and water in a blender. Purée until smooth. Press through a strainer into a small bowl, discarding the solids. Set the bowl over a saucepan of simmering water. Cook, stirring constantly until slightly thickened, about 6 minutes, making sure not to let it simmer. Stir in vanilla, lime juice and salt and pepper.

1 serving: 70 Calories; trace Total Fat (0 g Mono, 0 g Poly, 0 g Sat); 0 mg Cholesterol; 15 g Carbohydrate (2 g Fibre, 3 g Sugar); 2 g Protein; 10 mg Sodium

56

Cucumber Lime Green Tea Granita

Serves 4

In the midst of a summer heat wave, we're all looking for refreshment, and if you look to your garden, you won't need to look much farther than the nearest cucumber vine. The expression "cool as a cucumber" does not exist without good reason. But what to do with an abundance of cukes when it's too hot to make pickles? Do the opposite and turn them into granita. If you're skeptical at the thought of cucumbers as dessert, remember that among their closest relatives are melons. Besides, making granita is the perfect excuse to spend a few minutes out of every 30 standing in front of an open freezer.

2 cups (500 mL) water

1/2 cup (125 mL) sugar

zest from 2 limes

1 cup (250 mL) loosely packed fresh mint leaves

1 bag of green tea

3 cups (750 mL) peeled, seeded and chopped cucumber

juice from 1 lime

Combine water, sugar and lime zest in a medium saucepan. Bring to a boil and cook, stirring occasionally, until sugar has dissolved. Add mint leaves and tea bag and remove from heat. Cover and set aside to steep for 8 minutes, then remove cover and let cool to room temperature. Once cool, press through a fine-mesh sieve into a shallow, wide freezer-safe container with a tight-fitting lid. Discard the solids.

Meanwhile, purée cucumber in a blender (or with a hand blender) until smooth. Add to the container and stir to combine thoroughly with syrup mixture. Cover and transfer the container to the freezer for 1 hour.

Remove mixture from the freezer and stir with a fork, moving any ice crystals from the edges toward the centre and breaking up any large clumps of ice. Cover and return mixture to the freezer. Repeat every 30 minutes until all of mixture has turned into ice crystals. If the granita gets too hard to stir, leave it at room temperature for a few minutes before stirring. Once completely frozen, leave it in the freezer until serving time, then spoon into glasses and serve immediately.

1 serving: 120 Calories; 0 g Total Fat (0 g Mono, 0 g Poly, 0 g Sat); 0 mg Cholesterol; 31 g Carbohydrate (3 g Fibre, 27 g Sugar); 1 g Protein; 10 mg Sodium

Crunchy Cucumber Sushi Rolls

Serves 4 to 8 as an appetizer

Grow seedless-type cucumbers for these tasty rolls, which incorporate all the elements of real sushi, except the cucumber replaces the traditional nori. Sushi rice is now available at most grocery stores.

1 cup (250 mL) sushi rice

2 cups (500 mL) water, plus more for rinsing

2 1/2 Tbsp (37 mL) unseasoned rice vinegar

1 tsp (5 mL) sugar

1/4 tsp (1 mL) salt

2 to 3 medium seedless-type cucumbers

1 red pepper, sliced thinly lengthwise

1 avocado, pitted, peeled and sliced lengthwise 1/2 inch (12 mm) thick

1 Tbsp (15 mL) lime juice

soy sauce, for dipping

wasabi and pickled ginger, as desired

Measure rice into a medium saucepan. Add cool water to cover the rice by 1 inch (2.5 cm). Swirl the rice around in the pot vigorously with your hand, then pour off the water. Repeat 2 or 3 times, until the water is completely clear. Add 2 cups water. Bring to a boil over high heat, then cover and reduce heat to medium-low. Cook for 15 minutes, then turn stove off and let sit for 15 minutes.

Meanwhile, combine rice vinegar, sugar and salt in a small bowl and stir until sugar and salt dissolve. Once rice has finished cooking, transfer to a large stainless steel or glass bowl. While still hot, pour vinegar mixture over rice and stir gently to distribute evenly. Set rice aside, uncovered, to cool to room temperature. Rice can be made 3 to 4 hours ahead; store, covered with a damp kitchen towel, at room temperature. Do not refrigerate.

Beginning on one side, slice cucumbers very thinly lengthwise with a vegetable peeler. Discard the first 2 slices. When you reach the middle section of the cucumber, where the seeds are, turn the cucumber and begin slicing from the opposite side, again discarding the first 2 slices. Discard the centre section where the seeds are, or reserve for another use.

Toss the avocado slices with the lime juice as soon as you cut them.

Lay a sushi mat down on your work surface. Beginning 1 inch (2.5 cm) from the bottom edge, arrange cucumber slices widthwise on the mat, placing each slice so that it slightly overlaps the previous one. Working with wet hands, spread a 1/4 inch (6 mm) thick layer of rice evenly over the cucumber slices, leaving about 1 inch (2.5 cm) at the far end uncovered. About 1 inch (2.5 cm) from the bottom, place a row of avocado slices end to end across the rice. Lay a double row of red pepper slices on top of the avocado. Lift the bottom edge of the sushi mat and fold it over the fillings with a rolling motion. Roll all the way to the end using light, even pressure. When you reach the end, press the front and back sides firmly between your hands to firm up and seal the roll. Let the mat fall away and use scissors to trim any excess cucumber slices from the roll. Use a sharp knife to cut the roll into 6 to 8 slices. Repeat to form more rolls with remaining ingredients. Serve immediately with pickled ginger on the side and a small dish of soy sauce for dipping, with a dab of wasabi for diners to mix into the soy sauce to their preference.

1 serving: 300 Calories; 8 g Total Fat (4.5 g Mono, 1 g Poly, 1 g Sat); 0 mg Cholesterol; 53 g Carbohydrate (6 g Fibre, 6 g Sugar); 5 g Protein; 150 mg Sodium

Dill and Smoked Salmon Croquettes

Serves 4

Dill is another one of my favourite garden herbs, with its fresh, pungent scent and its delicate yellow and green umbels. It's a classic with fish, potatoes, eggs or borscht and an essential element for pickling, but its flavour is so distinctive that it often gets overlooked in favour of herbs that play better with others. But it can work very well combined with other herbs, as in our Spanakopita recipe (p. 132), for example, where it's mixed with oregano to add a subtle but essential herbal accent. In the dill and curry crème fraîche that accompanies these tasty croquettes, dill is paired with sweet and smoky double smoked salmon.

vegetable oil, as needed, for frying

4 oz (113 g) double smoked or candied salmon, chopped

1/2 cup (125 mL) chopped dill

1/4 cup (60 mL) thinly sliced green onion

zest and juice from 1 lemon

salt and black pepper to taste

1 egg

1 egg white

1/4 cup (60 mL) panko crumbs

Place at least 3/4 inch (2 cm) of vegetable oil in a large, heavy saucepan. Preheat over medium-high. Combine salmon, dill, onion, lemon zest and juice, salt and pepper in a medium bowl. Mix well. Add egg and egg white and mix until thoroughly incorporated.

Use 2 spoons to form mixture into 2 Tbsp (30 mL) patties. Pour panko crumbs onto a plate and coat patties on all sides. Working in batches, place patties into oil. Fry until golden and cooked through, 2 to 3 minutes on each side. Remove with a slotted spoon and drain on a baking sheet lined with paper towel. Arrange on plates or a platter and serve immediately with Dill and Curry Crème Fraîche on the side for dipping.

1 serving: 120 Calories; 4.5 g Total Fat (2.5 g Mono, 1 g Poly, 1 g Sat); 65 mg Cholesterol; 4 g Carbohydrates (0 g Fibre, 0 g Sugar); 14 g Protein; 530 mg Sodium

Combine cream and yogurt in a sterile glass jar. Mix well and cover tightly. Let sit overnight or 12 hours in a warm place to thicken. Stir in dill and curry. Keep in the refrigerator up to 3 days.

1/4 cup (60 mL): 150 Calories; 15 g Total Fat (4.5 g Mono, 0 g Poly, 9 g Sat); 55 mg Cholesterol; 3 g Carbohydrates (trace Fibre, 1 g Sugar); 2 g Protein; 25 mg Sodium

Don't grow dill near fennel because they will crosspollinate, and the seeds of both plants will lose their distinct flavours. Pick dill leaves as needed throughout summer and dry them for use in winter. Harvest the seeds by shaking the seedheads over a sheet once they ripen in late summer or fall.

Dill and Curry Crème Fraîche

3/4 cup (175 mL) whipping cream

1/4 cup (60 mL) plain yogurt with active cultures

3 Tbsp (45 mL) chopped fresh dill

1 Tbsp (15 mL) curry powder

Grilled Eggplant "Napoleons"

Serves 4 as an appetizer

Though eggplants can be tough to grow in parts of Canada, the sight of orbs of white, nearly black or any shade of purple dangling from the vine in your garden is well worth the effort. The fruit of your labour will be evident in the eating as well. If possible, use eggplants the same day you harvest them—they deteriorate quickly. If you must, store eggplants at room temperature two to three days at most; refrigerating them will make eggplants develop brown spots and turn bitter. If you usually salt eggplants to remove bitterness, you won't need to do that with those you grow in your own garden, because that bitterness is usually a result of storage that is too long or too cold.

2 small or 1 medium eggplant, sliced lengthwise 1/2 inch (12 mm) thick

2 red bell peppers, cut lengthwise into quarters

1/4 cup (60 mL) grape seed oil

1 block Haloumi cheese, sliced lengthwise into 8 pieces

1 lemon (ends discarded) sliced into 8 rounds *each* about 1/4 inch (6 mm) thick

Oregano Caper Dressing (see opposite)

2 Tbsp (30 mL) chopped fresh oregano

2 Tbsp (30 mL) basil chiffonade (see Tip, p. 15)

Preheat grill to medium-high. Lightly brush eggplant slices and pepper quarters on both sides with grape seed oil. Place in a single layer on the grill. Cook 2 to 3 minutes, carefully turn over and grill until second side is grill-marked and everything is just tender, about 2 minutes more. Transfer to a plate. Stack on each of 4 plates as follows: a slice of eggplant on the bottom, then a slice of lemon, a piece of pepper and a slice of cheese; repeat this sequence once more; then top with one last slice of eggplant. Drizzle dressing over all and sprinkle with oregano and basil. Serve immediately.

1 serving: 540 Calories; 45 g Total Fat (20 g Mono, 12 g Poly, 4 g Sat); 0 mg Cholesterol; 19 g Carbohydrate (9 g Fibre, 5 g Sugar); 19 g Protein; 280 mg Sodium

Combine all ingredients in a blender (or use a bowl and a hand blender), and purée until the solids are chopped into small bits but are not yet a uniform paste.

2 Tbsp (30 mL): 100 Calories; 11 g Total Fat (8 g Mono, 1 g Poly, 1.5 g Sat); 0 mg Cholesterol; 2 g Carbohydrates; 1 g Fibre; 0 g Sugar; 0 g Protein; 140 mg Sodium

Harvest eggplants when their skin is glossy and the flesh yields to gentle pressure but bounces back, regardless of size. Cut the stem just above the cap and be gentle, as they bruise easily.

Oregano Caper Dressing

6 Tbsp (90 mL) extra virgin olive oil

2 Tbsp (30 mL) lemon juice

1/4 cup (60 mL) chopped fresh oregano

2 Tbsp (30 mL) small capers, drained and rinsed

1/4 tsp (1 mL) salt

1/2 tsp (2 mL) black pepper

Fennel and Orange-stuffed Trout en Papillote

Serves 4

Who can resist the lure of fennel, with its delicate, feathery foliage in bright green and bronze varieties and its light licorice scent? The fronds are delicious sprinkled over fish or eggs or added to a vinaigrette or a marinade. If you grow Florence fennel, it can be braised until tender, sliced thinly and grilled to bring out its sweetness, or shaved raw and crunchy into salads and slaws. Here its flavour infuses the fish while the fennel is cooked until tender inside the envelope of parchment. If you don't grow Florence fennel, substitute 1/2 cup (125 mL) chopped fennel fronds for the sliced bulb.

2 cloves garlic, minced

1 small shallot, minced

2 Tbsp (30 mL) toasted fennel seed

2 tsp (10 mL) crushed red pepper flakes

1/2 tsp (2 mL) salt

1 tsp (5 mL) black pepper

4 x 10 oz (280 g) whole trout, cleaned and drawn

1 bulb fennel, white part thinly sliced, fronds reserved

1 orange, with peel, thinly sliced

Combine garlic, shallot, fennel, pepper flakes, salt and pepper in a small bowl. Cut 4 pieces of parchment large enough so that when folded in half they will leave a 2 inch (5 cm) border around the fish on all sides. Fold in half and crease the fold. Lay 1 fish on each piece of paper. Sprinkle fish inside and out with the spice mix. Lay a few slices of fennel inside each fish cavity, layer 2 to 3 orange slices atop the fennel, and add a few more fennel slices on top. Fold and roll the edges of the parchment to seal. Chill in refrigerator 2 hours for flavours to penetrate.

Preheat oven to 400°F (200°C). Arrange packages in a single layer on a baking sheet. Bake 15 minutes without turning. Transfer to serving plates. Open the parcels at the table (be careful of escaping steam) and garnish with reserved fennel fronds.

1 serving: 150 Calories; 6 g Total Fat (2 g Mono, 1.5 g Poly, 1 g Sat); 50 mg Cholesterol; 12 g Carbohydrate (4 g Fibre, 4 g Sugar); 20 g Protein; 320 mg Sodium

Harvest fennel leaves as needed for fresh use. The seeds can be harvested when ripe, in late summer or fall. Shake the seedheads over a sheet to collect the seeds. Let them dry thoroughly before storing them. Florence fennel can be harvested as soon as the bulbous base becomes swollen. Pull plants up as needed, and harvest any left in the ground before the first fall frost.

Floral Salad with Nasturtium Vinaigrette

Serves 4 to 6

Though we'll easily eat fruits and vegetables or leafy greens, for some reason we tend to draw the line at flowers. A few sneak into our diets here and there—artichokes, capers, broccoli—but we're very reluctant to eat flowers in any colour other than green (or coloured icing, but that's another matter). Flowers of many of our edibles are delectable in their own right, often tasting like a slightly milder version of the greens or fruits, like the flowers of many herbs such as cilantro, dill, basil or mint. But some flowers come as a pleasant shock to the senses: delicately scented rose petals surprise with a burst of citrus-like flavour on the tongue, and nasturtiums bring a peppery bite wherever they're used. The best way to familiarize yourself with the variety of flavours is to taste your way through your garden, nibbling on petals here and there— just don't sample any poisonous blooms. Eat only organic flowers—otherwise the concentration of pesticides or fertilizers present can be much stronger during flowering.

2 Tbsp (30 mL) extra virgin olive oil

1 Tbsp (15 mL) hazelnut oil

1 Tbsp (15 mL) honey

1 Tbsp (15 mL) white wine vinegar

4 nasturtium flowers

1 tsp (5 mL) lemon zest

pinch of salt

3 cups (750 g) mixed salad greens

1 cup (250 mL) sunflower sprouts

1 cup (250 mL) edible flowers (see list, opposite)

1/4 cup (60 mL) toasted sunflower seeds

For the vinagrette, combine oils, honey, vinegar, flowers, lemon zest and salt in a blender (or a small bowl and use a hand blender). Purée until smooth.

Combine greens, sprouts and flowers in a large bowl. Drizzle vinaigrette over and toss to coat. Sprinkle with sunflower seeds and serve immediately.

1 serving: 160 Calories; 12 g Total Fat (6 g Mono, 4 g Poly, 1.5 g Sat); 0 mg Cholesterol; 10 g Carbohydrate (1 g Fibre, 4 g Sugar); 4 g Protein; 15 mg Sodium

A brief list of edible flowers:

African violet
Apple (and other tree
fruit, including apricot,
peach, pear)
Aster
Beebalm
Calendula
Carnation
Chives
Chrysanthemum
    (tips only)
Clover
Cornflower
Dandelion
Daylily
Fuschia
Gardenia
Gladiola
Hibiscus

Hollyhock
Honeysuckle
Icelandic poppy
Lavender
Lilac
Okra
Pansy
Passion flower
Pea (but not sweet pea,
    which is toxic)
Peony
Pinks (sweet William)
Radish
Rose
Squash (including
zucchini and pumpkin)
Strawberry
Violet

Plum Clafoutis

Serves 8

Plums tend to be less romanticized than most of their stone fruit relatives. Peaches and apricots are beloved in spite of or because of their fuzzy skins, and cherries' brief season is hotly anticipated each year, but plums never seem to get their due. Plums are a generous fruit—multiple varieties mature at different times, extending the harvest season, and when you bite into a ripe one, the slightly floral nectar runs down your chin just as decadently as with any other stone fruit. As with their cousins, you may end up scrambling for ways to use plums when a tree-full starts to ripen all at once. A clafoutis is among the simplest of desserts to make, and this one, made with plums, is as delectable as the original cherry version.

1 cup (250 mL) milk

1 vanilla bean, split

1/2 cup (125 mL) butter, plus more for greasing the pan

3 eggs

1/2 cup (125 mL) white sugar

pinch of salt

1 cup (250 mL) flour, sifted

10 plums, halved and pitted (or enough to fill the pan)

confectioner's sugar, for garnish

Pour the milk into a small saucepan. Scrape the seeds from the vanilla bean into the milk, then drop the pod in. Bring almost to a boil over medium heat. Stir in butter. Once the butter has melted, remove from heat.

In a medium bowl, lightly beat the eggs. Add sugar and salt and beat until the mixture lightens in colour. Add flour all at once and beat until well mixed. Remove the vanilla pod from the milk and slowly pour in milk, beating constantly, until batter is smooth and shiny. Set aside to rest for 30 minutes.

Preheat oven to 400°F (200°C). Grease the bottom and sides of a 9 inch (23 cm) round cake pan. Arrange plums skin side up in the pan. Re-whisk batter if necessary and pour over plums. Bake until batter is golden brown on top and almost but not quite set in the middle, 30 to 40 minutes. Let sit for 15 minutes, then turn out onto a plate and sprinkle with confectioner's sugar to serve.

1 serving: 280 Calories; 14 g Total Fat (4 g Mono, 1 g Poly, 8 g Sat); 110 mg Cholesterol; 2 g Carbohydrate (2 g Fibre, 22 g Sugar); 5 g Protein; 105 mg Sodium

A mature plum tree can easily deliver 20 to 55 lbs (10 to 25 kg) of fruit. Plums are usually ready to harvest in late summer or early fall, but some varieties may ripen sooner. Basically if the fruit is plump and is easily plucked from the tree, it is ready to harvest.

Apple and Croissant Strata with Pecan Crumble

Serves 6 to 8

Some people regard an apple tree on their property as a nuisance—it drops fruit everywhere and generally makes a mess. But it all depends on the type of apple the tree produces. Some apples are mealy and flavourless, better suited to pressing for juice or cooking down into applesauce. Others are divine, crisp and juicy, sweet or tart. As long as they're good eaten out of hand, either sweet or tart apples will work in this breakfast treat. Throw it together the night before, then just sprinkle on the topping and pop it in the oven in the morning for a decadent brunch that you need only barely get out of bed to make.

5 Tbsp (75 mL) chilled butter, *divided*

juice from 1 lemon

4 medium apples

6 day-old croissants, cut into 1 inch (2.5 cm) pieces

8 oz (250 g) cream cheese, cut into 1/2 inch (12 mm) dice

6 eggs, beaten

1 3/4 cups (425 mL) milk

(see next page)

Use 1 Tbsp (15 mL) butter to grease a 2 quart (2 L) casserole dish. Place lemon juice in a medium bowl. Peel, core and cut apples into 1/2 inch (12 mm) dice, and toss with lemon juice immediately. Spread a quarter of the croissant pieces in the bottom of the prepared dish. Top with a third of the apples, then a third of the cheese. Repeat this pattern twice, then top with a final layer of croissant pieces. In a medium bowl, whisk together eggs, milk, sugar, vanilla, 1/2 tsp (2 mL) cinnamon and nutmeg. Pour evenly over the strata. Cover tightly and refrigerate at least 8 hours and up to 1 day.

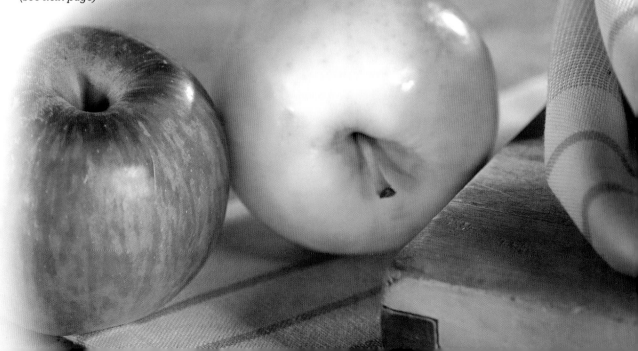

Remove strata from refrigerator and let stand at room temperature 30 minutes. Preheat oven to 350°F (175°C).

Cut up remaining 4 Tbsp (60 mL) butter into small pieces. Combine flour, brown sugar and remaining 1 tsp (5 mL) cinnamon in the bowl of a food processor or a medium bowl. Add butter and pulse or cut in until the mixture resembles coarse crumbs. Stir in the nuts. The streusel could also be made the night before and kept covered and refrigerated until needed. Sprinkle over strata. Bake until puffed and cooked through (a knife inserted into the centre should come out clean), about 45 minutes. Let stand 10 minutes before serving, then serve warm.

1 serving: 590 Calories; 31 g Total Fat (11 g Mono, 4.5 g Poly, 12 g Sat); 210 mg Cholesterol; 65 g Carbohydrate (5 g Fibre, 39 g Sugar); 17 g Protein; 20 mg Sodium

1/4 cup (60 mL) sugar

1/2 tsp (2 mL) vanilla

1 1/2 tsp (7 mL) cinnamon, *divided*

1/4 tsp (1 mL) nutmeg

1/3 cup (75 mL) all-purpose flour

1/2 cup (125 mL) packed brown sugar

1 cup (250 mL) chopped pecans

Roasted Garlic Spiral Rolls

Makes 12 buns

Garlic is easy to grow and doesn't take up much space in the garden; its leaves (called scapes) can be picked throughout the season to add a mild garlic flavour to a variety of dishes; and at harvest time, you'll pull fragrant bulbs fresh from the soil. Elephant garlic has a much milder flavour. If you haven't tried roasting garlic, you're missing out. Even if you find it sharp and less than appealing in its raw state, you'll be seduced by the luscious texture and mellow sweetness of roasted garlic. It's good enough to spread on toast and eat as is, but here we've spread it onto dough and rolled it up for a savoury take on cinnamon buns.

Dough

1 1/4 cups (300 mL) lukewarm (105°F, 41°C) water

2 tsp (10 mL) honey

4 tsp (20 mL) active dry yeast

3 cups (750 mL) flour

1 1/2 tsp (7 mL) salt

1/4 cup (60 mL) extra virgin olive oil, plus extra for oiling the bowl and dough

(see next page)

Combine lukewarm water and honey in a small bowl and stir until dissolved. Sprinkle the yeast overtop and set aside to bloom for 10 to 15 minutes. In the bowl of a mixer fitted with the paddle attachment or a large bowl, combine flour and salt. Mix well. Add olive oil to water/yeast mixture and stir to combine well. Mixing on low speed, add liquids to flour. Continue mixing until all the flour is absorbed. Remove the paddle attachment and fit the mixer with the dough hook. Mix at medium speed for 5 to 7 minutes. The dough should come together to form a smooth ball. Shape into a ball and place in a large, oiled mixing bowl. Turn over, so all sides of dough are lightly coated with oil. Cover with a damp dishtowel and set aside in a warm place until doubled in size, 30 to 45 minutes.

Meanwhile, place roasted garlic in a blender or small bowl. Add anchovies, if using, thyme and pepper, and purée until smooth.

Turn dough out onto a lightly floured work surface. Punch down, then roll out into a 14 x 10 inch (35 x 25 cm) rectangle. Spread garlic mixture over dough all the way to the edges. Sprinkle olives over top. Roll up lengthwise, jelly-roll-style. Cut crosswise in 1 inch (2.5 cm) wide slices. Transfer to greased baking sheet in a single layer, leaving space between them. Lightly brush the tops and sides of buns with oil. Cover with a damp dishtowel and set aside in a warm place until doubled in size, about 30 minutes. Preheat oven to 375°F (190°C). Uncover and bake until golden, about 30 to 40 minutes. Serve warm or at room temperature.

1 bun: 180 Calories; 3.5 g Total Fat (2.5 g Mono, 0 g Poly, 0 g Sat); 0 mg Cholesterol; 33 g Carbohydrate (7 g Fibre, 1 g Sugar); 5 g Protein; 340 mg Sodium

Tip

To roast garlic, preheat the oven to 350°F (175°C). Slice the top off each bulb of garlic to expose the cloves, and lay them cut side up in a baking dish. Drizzle with olive oil and sprinkle with salt. Roast 20 to 30 minutes or until cloves are tender. Remove from oven and set aside until cool enough to handle. Squeeze the buttery flesh of the cloves out of the bulb, and discard the papery skin.

Filling

6 heads roasted garlic (or 2 heads roasted elephant garlic), see Tip

6 anchovy fillets, optional

2 Tbsp (30 mL) chopped fresh thyme

1 tsp (5 mL) black pepper

1/2 cup (125 mL) drained and coarsely chopped Niçoise olives

Greens and Goat Cheese Quesadillas

Serves 6 as an appetizer

Kale, collards and mustard greens tend to be among the most prolific plants in my garden, and I sometimes have a hard time keeping up. Luckily, the greens of the brassica family are also among the most nutritious plants in the garden, so it's well worth seeking out a variety of ways to enjoy them. Here, in combination with tangy goat cheese, peppery (if you choose to go with mustard greens) or mildly bitter (if you choose kale or collards) greens bring a new flavour profile to quesadillas. These tasty morsels can be a little messy to make, but their taste will be your reward.

1 Tbsp (15 mL) grape seed oil

2 cloves garlic, minced

4 cups (1 L) plus 2/3 cup (150 mL) coarsely chopped greens, stems removed, *divided*

1 1/3 cups (325 mL) Salsa Verde (see p. 110)

4 x 8 inch (20 cm) whole wheat tortillas

(see next page)

Place a baking sheet in the oven and preheat to 275°F (140°C). Heat grape seed oil in a large sauté pan over medium. Add garlic and cook, stirring, until fragrant, about 1 minute. Add 4 cups (1 L) of greens. Cook, stirring, until lightly wilted, about 3 minutes. Remove from heat and set aside.

Combine salsa and remaining greens in a food processor; blend until greens are finely chopped.

Lay tortillas on a work surface. Place potato slices in a large bowl and sprinkle with chili powder, salt and pepper; toss to coat. Mix in Jack cheese. Place a quarter of the wilted

greens on half of each tortilla. Divide potato mixture among tortillas, placing on top of greens. Add goat cheese and 2 Tbsp (30 mL) salsa mixture to each tortilla half. Fold uncovered tortilla halves over filling and press firmly. Brush top half with oil.

Heat a large, non-stick sauté pan over medium. Place 2 quesadillas, oiled side down, in pan. Brush tops with oil. Cook until lightly browned, about 3 minutes. Flip carefully and brown the other side. Transfer to baking sheet in oven to keep warm. Repeat with remaining quesadillas. Cut each quesadilla into 3 or 4 wedges and serve with remaining salsa.

1 serving: 440 Calories; 21 g Total Fat (5 g Mono, 4.5 g Poly, 8 g Sat); 35 mg Cholesterol; 50 g Carbohydrate (8 g Fibre, 3 g Sugar); 18 g Protein; 640 mg Sodium

2 medium yellow-fleshed potatoes cut into 1/2 inch (12 mm) dice, cooked (about 1 cup, 250 mL)

2 tsp (10 mL) chili powder

salt and black pepper to taste

1 1/3 cups (325 mL) packed coarsely grated Monterey Jack cheese (about 5 oz, 140 g)

3 oz (85 g) chilled fresh goat cheese, coarsely crumbled

Horseradish and Lime Burgers and Sauce

Serves 4

A freshly dug horseradish root is quite mild, but once grated or ground, it has a sharp, tingling bite that goes from your tongue through your nose straight to your brain. Horseradish is exhilarating; it awakens the palate and all the senses and makes every flavour stand out in sharp relief. When the root's cells are crushed, they release isothicyanate, a volatile oil that gives horseradish its characteristic flavour. Mixing horseradish with an acid such as vinegar, or in this case, lime juice, stops the reaction, and the point at which the acid is added determines its potency (the sooner you add it, the stronger the sauce will be). In prepared sauces, horseradish's bite can be lessened by lack of freshness or too many other ingredients; make your own, and you control the result.

1/3 cup (75 mL) freshly grated horseradish (see Tip)

1 Tbsp (15 mL) lime juice

1 tsp (5 mL) lime zest

1/2 tsp (2 mL) *each* coarse salt and black pepper

1/2 cup (125 mL) whipping cream

1 lb (454 g) lean ground beef

4 fresh hamburger-type buns

4 leaves lettuce

1 tomato, sliced

1 avocado, pitted, peeled and sliced

1/4 red onion, sliced

Mix grated horseradish immediately with the lime juice to retain its full flavour. Add zest, salt and pepper and mix well. In a separate bowl, whip the whipping cream to soft peaks. Fold into horseradish mixture and set aside.

Preheat grill to high. Place ground beef in a large mixing bowl. Add half the horseradish mixture, reserving the other half. Mix well. Divide beef mixture into 4 balls and form into thick patties. Grill patties about 4 to 6 minutes per side until an instant-read thermometer inserted into the centre registers 160°F (71°C). In the last few minutes of cooking, add the buns, cut side down, to the grill and toast lightly. Serve immediately topped with lettuce, tomato, avocado and remaining sauce.

1 serving: 570 Calories; 34 g Total Fat (15 g Mono, 2.5 g Poly, 14 g Sat); 100 mg Cholesterol; 32 g Carbohydrate (6 g Fibre, 6 g Sugar); 29 g Protein; 620 mg Sodium

Tip

A microplane is the best tool for grating fresh horseradish.

When the horseradish foliage dies back in autumn, you can dig up some of the roots to use fresh or in preserves, relishes and pickles. The roots have the strongest flavour in autumn, but they can be harvested at any time once the plant is well established.

Quick-pickled Kohlrabi

Makes about 2 cups (500 mL)

I absolutely love to grow anything that's slightly strange and unusual. If there's a chance that someone might think it is "novelty produce," count me in. Kohlrabi falls into this category because of its unusual, intriguing shape. It's not exactly a novelty, though: the emperor Charlemagne, who ruled in the 7th century AD, ordered kohlrabi to be grown in his lands. Milder than many other members of the brassica family, it is a versatile vegetable. Kohlrabi is wonderful raw, either thinly sliced or grated into a slaw; it can be steamed, stir-fried, braised, grilled and roasted. The leaves are edible, too; treat them as you would kale or collards. Here, we make the most of kohlrabi's crunchiness and nutty flavour in a quick pickle for those who love a good pickle but can't stand to wait.

3/4 lb (340 g) kohlrabi, trimmed

3/4 tsp (4 mL) salt

3 to 4 fresh curry leaves, optional

1/2 cup (125 mL) champagne vinegar

1/2 cup (125 mL) white cranberry juice

1 tsp (5 mL) whole coriander seeds

1/2 tsp (2 mL) brown mustard seeds

zest of 1/2 lemon, cut in strips

1 x 2 cup (500 mL) sterile glass jar with lid and sealing ring

Use a mandoline to slice kohlrabi crosswise about 1/4 inch (6 mm) thick. Place in a medium bowl and toss with salt. Set aside to rest at room temperature about 1 hour. Drain and pack into a sterile glass jar. Add curry leaves, if using.

Combine vinegar, cranberry juice, coriander, mustard seeds and lemon zest in a small saucepan. Bring to a boil, then pour over kohlrabi. Cover and cool to room temperature before transferring to refrigerator. Store in refrigerator at least 2 days, and up to 3 weeks, before eating.

1/4 cup (60 mL): 25 Calories; 0 g Total Fat (0 g Mono, 0 g Poly, 0 g Sat); 0 mg Cholesterol; 5 g Carbohydrate (2 g Fibre, 3 g Sugar); trace Protein; 230 mg Sodium

Keep a close eye on your kohlrabi because the bulb can become tough and woody quickly if left too long before harvesting. The bulb is generally well rounded and 2 to 4 inches (5 to 10 cm) in diameter when ready for harvesting. Pull up the entire plant and cut just below the bulb, then cut the leaves and stems off and compost them or use them to mulch the bed.

Pork Chops with Creamed Balsamic Leeks

Serves 4

Among the most beautiful of all the onions grown in the garden, leeks are also the most versatile. Their flavour is milder and more subtle than that of onions, and their green colour brings extra nutrients to the table. They have been cultivated and consumed since the 2nd millennium BC, and they have staying power in the garden—they'll be fine until the ground freezes, even under a blanket of snow. Creamed leeks are a classic with pork chops, but a little white balsamic vinegar adds a whole new layer of flavour.

2 tsp (10 mL) grape seed oil

4 boneless pork loin chops

1/2 tsp (2 mL) *each* salt and black pepper

2 Tbsp (30 mL) butter

6 leeks, cleaned well and cut lengthwise into 1/2 inch (12 mm) wide strips

1/4 cup (60 mL) white balsamic vinegar

2 Tbsp (30 mL) whipping cream

Heat oil in a large sauté pan over medium-high. Sprinkle pork chops on both sides with salt and pepper. Add chops to pan and cook until golden brown and just barely pink inside, 3 to 4 minutes on each side. Transfer to a cutting board and tent loosely with foil to rest.

Meanwhile, melt butter in a large sauté pan over medium-low. Add leeks and cook, stirring occasionally, until they begin to soften, about 5 minutes. Add the balsamic vinegar and remaining salt and pepper; cook until reduced by half, about 5 minutes more. Stir in cream and cook just to heat through. Divide into 4 equal portions. Pile most of each portion of leeks on a serving plate, lean a pork chop on top and pile remaining leeks on top of that.

1 serving: 400 Calories; 25 g Total Fat (9 g Mono, 3.5 g Poly, 10 g Sat); 85 mg Cholesterol; 21 g Carbohydrate (4 g Fibre, 7 g Sugar); 22 g Protein; 400 mg Sodium

Tip

Leeks need to be washed well—slice them lengthwise and run them under the tap so the water washes away the gritty dirt that might have accumulated in the layers.

Leeks can be harvested as soon as they are mature in early autumn, but because they are so hardy, you can just harvest them as you need them until the ground begins to freeze. At that point you should pull up any you want for winter use. They keep for several weeks in the refrigerator if you cut the roots short and wrap the leeks in plastic. For longer storage, they can be frozen. Be sure to double bag them so the onion-like flavour doesn't seep into any other food you have in the freezer.

Mesclun Mix with Cherries, Fennel and Goat Cheese

Serves 4

Depending on where in Canada you live, lettuce greens can be easy or not-so-easy to grow. In places where the summer is hot, the lettuce leaves are too small to pick and eat one day, and the next they've already bolted and turned suddenly bitter. But no kitchen garden is complete without a row or two or a patch of lettuce. If there's one thing you can rely on, it's that within a few weeks of planting, you'll have small colourful lettuce leaves. And the possibilities in those leaves are endless. This version celebrates the early lettuce crop, combining it with cherries—the first of the stone fruits—fennel and almond-crusted fresh goat cheese.

2 Tbsp (30 mL) extra virgin olive oil

1 Tbsp (15 mL) lemon juice

zest from 1 lemon

2 tsp (10 mL) honey

1/4 tsp (1 mL) salt

1/2 tsp (2 mL) cracked black pepper

1/3 cup (75 mL) toasted flaked almonds

4 oz (113 g) goat cheese

1 fennel bulb, outer leaves and root trimmed

4 cups (1 L) mesclun mix

1 cup (250 mL) halved, pitted cherries

Combine olive oil, lemon juice and zest, honey, salt and pepper in a small bowl. Whisk thoroughly.

Place almonds on a plate. Cut goat cheese into 4 rounds and press into the almonds to coat on all sides.

Slice fennel lengthwise as thinly as possible (use a mandoline if you have one). Transfer to a large bowl. Add mesclun mix and cherries. Drizzle dressing over, reserving 2 Tbsp (30 mL). Toss to coat. Divide among 4 plates. Top salad on each plate with a round of goat cheese and drizzle remaining dressing over the cheese. Serve immediately.

1 serving: 240 Calories; 18 g Total Fat (10 g Mono, 2 g Poly, 3 g Sat); 15 mg Cholesterol; 16 g Carbohydrate (4 g Fibre, 8 g Sugar); 9 g Protein; 290 mg Sodium

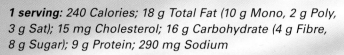

Head-forming lettuce can be harvested once the head is plump. If the weather turns very hot, you may wish to cut heads even earlier because the leaves develop a bitter flavour once plants go to flower. Looseleaf lettuce and mesclun can be harvested by pulling a few leaves off as needed or by cutting an entire plant 2 to 4 inches (5 to 10 cm) above ground level. Most will continue to produce new leaves when cut this way.

Southwestern Lettuce Wraps

Serves 4

Lettuce has been relegated to the salad bowl for too long. Have you ever considered that the lettuce growing in your garden just might be the perfect finger food? Crunchy, yet flexible butter lettuce makes an ideal vehicle for transporting other food from plate to mouth. As a wrap, it has many advantages over flour- or corn-based wraps—it's less filling, doesn't get soggy and adds crunch. Asian flavours are cropping up in lettuce wraps all over restaurant menus and are delicious to make at home, but we took ours in a different direction with the flavours of the Southwest.

3 Tbsp (45 mL) grape seed oil

1 Tbsp (15 mL) lime juice

1 tsp (5 mL) lime zest

1/2 tsp (2 mL) cumin

1/4 tsp (1 mL) chili powder

1/4 tsp (1 mL) oregano

1/4 tsp (1 mL) salt

1/4 tsp (1 mL) black pepper

2 chicken breasts

1 to 2 heads butter lettuce, depending on size, leaves separated

1 avocado, pitted, peeled and thinly sliced

1 red pepper, thinly sliced

(see next page)

Combine grape seed oil, lime juice and zest, cumin, chili powder, oregano, salt and pepper in a shallow dish. Add chicken breasts and turn once to coat. Cover and refrigerate for 2 to 3 hours, turning occasionally.

Preheat oven to 350°F (175°C). Drain chicken and discard marinade. Bake chicken until cooked through, 25 to 30 minutes. Set aside to cool. Chicken can be cooked up to 1 day ahead. Cover and refrigerate. Shred chicken breasts.

Into the cupped side of each lettuce leaf, place about 2 to 3 Tbsp (30 to 45 mL) shredded chicken breast, a few slices of avocado, a few slices of red pepper, 1 to 2 Tbsp (15 to 30 mL) black beans and a sprinkling each of cheese and green onion. Serve with salsa on the side.

1 serving: 430 Calories; 25 g Total Fat (8 g Mono, 9 g Poly, 4.5 g Sat); 85 mg Cholesterol; 19 g Carbohydrate (9 g Fibre, 4 g Sugar); 36 g Protein; 400 mg Sodium

1/2 cup (125 mL) black beans

1/2 cup (125 mL) grated Monterey Jack cheese

1/4 cup (60 mL) thinly sliced green onion

salsa, as needed

Prawn and Melon Verrine

Serves 4

Melons can be difficult to grow in Canada—they need a longer, hotter season than most parts of the country can give. But that doesn't mean it can't be done, and it's definitely worth trying if you have the room. No success tastes sweeter than the juice of a melon grown in your own backyard. We've used a combination of melons in this sweet/savoury dish, but you could use only a single variety if you like. The term "verrine" is a play on the idea of a terrine; the layers are contained in a glass, and *verre* is French for glass.

1 honeydew melon, peeled and seeded

1/2 cup honey

zest and juice from 4 limes, *divided*

juice from 2 lemons

1/3 cup (75 mL) fresh mint, finely chopped

2 Tbsp (30 mL) grape seed oil

splash of sesame oil

2 tsp (5 mL) sugar, plus more to taste

coarse sea salt and cayenne pepper to taste

1 avocado, pitted, peeled and cut in medium dice

1 lb (454 g) cooked prawns, peeled and deveined

1 cup (250 mL) cantaloupe, cut into bite-sized pieces

mint leaves for garnish

For the sauce, purée three quarters of the honeydew melon in a blender. Strain through a fine-mesh sieve into a small saucepan over medium heat. Discard the pulp. Add the honey and juice from 1 lime and reduce until syrupy, about 10 minutes. Stir in the sugar until dissolved. Cool the syrup in its pot over an ice water bath. When chilled, season to taste with salt, cayenne and juice from 1 lime. Refrigerate until ready to use.

Combine lemon juice, juice and zest from 2 limes, mint and grape seed and sesame oils in a medium bowl; mix thoroughly. Season to taste with sugar, salt and cayenne. Add avocado to the bowl immediately after cutting and toss to coat. Use a slotted spoon to divide avocado evenly among 4 chilled glasses.

Set 8 prawns aside and chop remaining prawns into bite-sized pieces. Cut remaining quarter of honeydew into bite-sized pieces. Add half of the chopped prawns to the dressing in the bowl and toss to coat. With the slotted spoon, divide prawns among the glasses, layering on top of the avocado. Repeat with half of the chopped honeydew, all of the cantaloupe, the remaining chopped prawns, and finally the remaining chopped honeydew. Top each glass with 2 whole prawns. Drizzle sauce evenly over the 4 glasses. Garnish each glass with a sprig of mint, if desired, and serve immediately.

1 serving: 430 Calories; 16 g Total Fat (7 g Mono, 7 g Poly, 2 g Sat); 220 mg Cholesterol; 54 g Carbohydrate (5 g Fibre, 45 g Sugar); 26 g Protein; 280 mg Sodium

Yogurt-marinated Lamb with Fresh Mint

Serves 4

Mint can be a dangerous plant to grow in the garden because it tends to run a little rampant. I've known plenty of people who will grow mint only in pots, or in a section of garden with its own underground brick wall, designed to prevent roots from spreading. But who can resist the seductions of mint, especially with the seemingly infinite varieties that are available to grow these days? Mint brings brightness and sparkle to any dish in which it is included, and you'll find it listed in the ingredients of many recipes in this book. For our feature mint recipe, we've used it in a classic pairing with lamb with an Indian-style yogurt marinade and spice rub.

1 Tbsp (15 mL) whole coriander seeds

1/2 Tbsp (7 mL) whole cumin seeds

1/2 Tbsp (7 mL) whole fennel seeds

1 tsp (5 mL) whole mustard seeds

1/2 green cardamom pod

1/2 tsp (2 mL) cinnamon

3/4 cup (175 mL) plain Balkan-style yogurt, drained

1/2 cup (125 mL) loosely packed fresh mint, plus sprigs for garnish

2 Tbsp (30 mL) lemon juice

1 Tbsp (15 mL) finely grated lemon zest

salt and black pepper to taste

12 x 1 inch (2.5 cm) thick lamb loin chops

grape seed oil

Combine coriander, cumin, fennel, mustard seeds and cardamom in a dry small sauté pan. Toast over medium heat, shaking constantly, until fragrant, about 1 minute. Remove from heat and stir in cinnamon. Spread on a large plate to cool.

Pull out cardamom and chop coarsely with a knife. Transfer cardamom and spice mixture to a spice grinder or mortar, and pulse or grind until the mixture has the texture of coarse cornmeal. Set aside

Combine yogurt, mint, lemon juice and zest in a food processor. Pulse briefly, just to blend. Add salt and pepper. Transfer half the mixture to a small bowl; cover and refrigerate.

Lay chops in a single layer in a shallow glass or ceramic dish. Spread both sides of the chops with the remaining yogurt mixture. Cover and refrigerate about 2 hours.

Preheat grill to medium-high. Spray grill lightly with grape seed oil. With a paper towel, wipe excess marinade from the lamb chops. Season on both sides with salt, pepper and 1 Tbsp (15 mL) spice rub.

Grill the chops to medium-rare, 1 to 2 minutes on each side. (If you prefer your lamb cooked more, grill for a little longer.) Transfer to a warm platter, tent loosely with foil and let rest 5 minutes.

Lightly sprinkle remaining spice rub over the chops. Garnish with mint sprigs and serve with reserved yogurt mixture on the side.

1 serving: 640 Calories; 51 g Total Fat (17 g Mono, 4.5 g Poly, 24 g Sat); 165 mg Cholesterol; 7 g Carbohydrate (3 g Fibre, 2 g Sugar); 36 g Protein; 400 mg Sodium

Sweet and Sour Okra with Grape Tomatoes

Serves 4

My father measures the progress of his garden by the height of his okra plants; if they don't reach 6 feet (2 metres) by mid-August, it must not be a very good year. I, on the other hand, have never had much luck with growing okra, perhaps because the hottest spot in my garden is perennially occupied by equally heat-seeking, sprawling melons instead of tall, stately okra with its lovely, hibiscus-like blooms. While I've never met anyone who objected to okra's flowers, many people object to its texture. Yes, okra can be slimy. Many dishes that use okra rely on that quality: gumbo is a case in point—okra's sliminess adds body to the broth. But okra doesn't have to be slimy. When cooked quickly by a dry heat method such as frying, roasting or grilling, the pods come out tender-crisp, with no sign of slime. Okra also seems to have a natural affinity for acidic flavours such as the pomegranate molasses and tomatoes in our recipe.

3 Tbsp (45 mL) grape seed oil

1 Tbsp (15 mL) pomegranate molasses

1 Tbsp (15 mL) brown sugar

1/2 tsp (2 mL) crushed red pepper

1/4 tsp (1 mL) salt

1/2 tsp (2 mL) cracked black pepper

1 lb (454 g) okra, trimmed

1 cup (250 mL) grape tomatoes

Preheat a large sauté pan over medium-high. Combine grape seed oil, pomegranate molasses, brown sugar, crushed red pepper, salt and pepper in a large bowl. Whisk thoroughly. Add okra and toss to coat. Transfer okra to pan and cook, stirring, until just beginning to become tender. Meanwhile, add the tomatoes to the leftover dressing in the bowl and toss to coat. Add tomatoes and dressing to the pan and cook, stirring, until okra are just tender-crisp and tomatoes are just beginning to blister and collapse, about 1 minute more.

1 serving: 160 Calories; 11 g Total Fat (2.5 g Mono, 8 g Poly, 1 g Sat); 0 mg Cholesterol; 17 g Carbohydrate (4 g Fibre, 9 g Sugar); 2 g Protein; 170 mg Sodium

Okra plants can be spiny, so it is best to wear gloves when harvesting the fruit. The fruit is picked when still immature, usually a week or two after the flower drops and the pod sets. Pods are usually harvested when they are about 3 to 4 cm (8 to 10 cm) long.

Roasted Onions Stuffed with Orzo "Mac 'n' Cheese"

Serves 4

Onions have been cultivated for more than 5000 years and are an essential ingredient in our cooking. Tricks to keep us from crying while we chop onions abound, but no one ever suggests that we avoid cooking with onions because of that inconvenience. The onion is, in fact, so firmly rooted in our cuisine that it is often said all one needs to do to create the illusion of a wondrous meal coming together in the kitchen is to set a pan of onions on the heat to fry. The sweet aroma wafting out of the kitchen is like a subconscious dinner bell ringing. Most often, however, onions play a supporting role, melding into a flavour base for a sauce or a stock, for example. Here, the onion takes centre stage: its luscious layers, caramelized into sweetness, envelope creamy pasta and cheese with a hint of smoke and a second layer of onion flavour.

4 large white onions

grape seed oil, as needed, for brushing

2 cups (500 mL) orzo

1/4 cup (60 mL) butter

1/4 cup (60 mL) flour

3 cloves garlic, minced

1 Tbsp (15 mL) minced shallots

1 1/2 cups (375 mL) white wine

1 1/2 cups (375 mL) milk

(see next page)

Preheat oven to 350°F (175°C). Trim onions at both ends and peel. Carefully carve out the inside layers of the onion, leaving 2 or 3 outer layers intact. Reserve the insides for another use (chop them up now so they're ready when you need them; mix them with a little oil and keep covered and refrigerated up to 1 week). Brush onion shells lightly inside and outside with oil. Transfer to a baking sheet and roast until golden and starting to collapse, about 30 minutes.

Bring a large pot of salted water to a boil. Add orzo and cook, stirring occasionally, until just shy of al dente, 5 to 6 minutes. Drain.

Meanwhile, melt butter in a large saucepan over medium-low. Add flour and cook, stirring constantly, about 1 minute. Add garlic and shallots and cook, still stirring constantly, another minute. Whisk in white wine. Bring to a simmer and cook, stirring occasionally, about 5 minutes. Add milk, return to a simmer and cook another 5 minutes. Remove from heat and stir in green onion and both cheeses. Stir until melted. Add orzo to sauce and mix well.

While cooking the pasta and cheese sauce, heat tomato sauce in a small saucepan over medium just until hot.

Preheat broiler. Spoon pasta and cheese mixture into onion shells. Broil until the top layer of pasta and cheese is brown and bubbling. Spoon about 1/4 cup (60 mL) of tomato sauce onto the centre of each of 4 plates. With a spatula, carefully transfer a stuffed onion to each plate. Serve immediately.

1 serving: 1000 Calories; 39 g Total Fat (11 g Mono, 4 g Poly, 22 g Sat); 110 mg Cholesterol; 105 g Carbohydrate (6 g Fibre, 22 g Sugar); 32 g Protein; 1090 mg Sodium

4 green onions, thinly sliced

1 1/2 cups (375 mL) smoked mozzarella

1 1/2 cups (375 mL) white Cheddar

1 cup (250 mL) Smoked Tomato Sauce (see p. 152)

Oregano-dressed Israeli Couscous Salad

Serves 4

Oregano, another member of the mint family that most of us couldn't live without, is one herb that most cooks use more often dried than fresh. When dried, it has a stronger impact, but when fresh it adds a light, bright herbal flavour. And if it's growing just steps from the kitchen, why wait until it shrivels up to use it? A natural paired with other Mediterranean flavours, oregano makes this variation on a pasta salad bright and summery, perfect to make ahead and take for lunch or carry to a picnic or potluck. Israeli couscous is simply a much larger grade of the familiar tiny grains of pasta, with its grains expanding to about the size of pearls when cooked. It has a heartier, more toothsome texture, making it a standout in warm and cold side dishes like this one. Look for it in the import aisle of your grocer or at specialty grocers. If you can't find it, substitute regular couscous and shorten the cooking time for a slightly different character.

1 Tbsp (15 mL) pomegranate molasses

1 Tbsp (15 mL) lemon juice

zest from 1 lemon

2 tsp (10 mL) honey

pinch of salt

1/4 tsp (1 mL) black pepper

1/4 cup (60 mL) extra virgin olive oil

1 cup (250 mL) uncooked Israeli couscous

1 tsp (5 mL) grape seed oil

(see next page)

For the dressing, combine first 6 ingredients in a small bowl. Whisk well. Slowly drizzle in the olive oil while whisking constantly.

Bring a large saucepan of salted water to a boil. Add Israeli couscous and cook, stirring occasionally, until al dente, 8 to 10 minutes. Drain, transfer to a large mixing bowl and toss with dressing, then set aside to cool to room temperature.

Meanwhile, heat oil in a large sauté pan over medium-high. Add zucchini and cook until tender-crisp and just starting to brown, 3 to 4 minutes. Remove from heat and set aside to cool. Once cool, add to couscous in mixing bowl. Add tomatoes, onion, oregano, caper berries and cheese

and toss to combine. If serving immediately, add the almonds and toss once again; if you'll be taking the salad somewhere, pack the almonds separately and add them at the last minute so they don't get soggy.

1 serving: *460 Calories; 23 g Total Fat (15 g Mono, 3 g Poly, 4 g Sat); 10 mg Cholesterol; 60 g Carbohydrate (11 g Fibre, 11 g Sugar); 11 g Protein; 300 mg Sodium*

These bushy perennials make lovely additions to any border and can be trimmed to form low hedges. The flowers attract pollinators and beneficial insects to the garden. Leaves can be picked as needed for fresh use or dried for use in winter.

2 medium zucchini, cut into 1/2 inch (12 mm) pieces

1 cup (250 mL) halved cherry or grape tomatoes

1/2 red onion, finely chopped

1/2 cup (125 mL) chopped fresh oregano

1/2 cup (125 mL) caper berries, rinsed and drained

1/2 cup (125 mL) crumbled feta cheese

1/4 cup (60 mL) toasted chopped almonds

Stir-fried Crab with Baby Bok Choy

Serves 4

The members of the brassica family that we classify as Oriental cabbages are, for the most part, milder than their European cousins. Suey choy, the large, light green variety (also known as Napa cabbage) is delicious both raw and cooked, while bok choy is most often cooked into a stir-fry, as it is here, where the green parts of the leaves wilt and become tender, and the fleshy white ribs remain tender-crisp. Marinating the crab before cooking allows the flavours to penetrate the meat, so you'll need to buy a whole live crab. Don't be intimidated; we'll walk you through the process (see Tip, opposite), and you'll taste the difference in the finished dish. Look for a crab that is lively, not slow-moving or listless.

3 Tbsp (45 mL) soy sauce, *divided*

3 Tbsp (45 mL) dry sherry, *divided*

4 Tbsp (60 mL) minced ginger, *divided*

1 live Dungeness crab, prepared as instructed (see Tip)

2 Tbsp (30 mL) grape seed oil

3 to 4 hot chili peppers, seeds and ribs removed, thinly sliced

1 Tbsp (15 mL) minced garlic

1/2 cup (125 mL) water

8 to 12 heads baby bok choy

1 tsp (5 mL) cornstarch

Combine 2 Tbsp (30 mL) soy sauce, 2 Tbsp (30 mL) sherry and 1 Tbsp (15 mL) ginger in a large bowl. Add crab pieces and toss to coat. Cover and refrigerate for 30 minutes.

Drain crab, reserving marinade. Heat oil in a wok or large sauté pan over medium-high. Add remaining ginger, chilies and garlic. Cook, stirring, until fragrant, about 30 seconds. Add crab pieces. Cook, stirring, until shells begin to turn red. Add reserved marinade, water and bok choy. Cover and cook, stirring every minute or so, until shells are entirely red, exposed meat is opaque and bok choy are just tender at the base, about 5 minutes.

Combine remaining soy sauce and sherry in a small bowl. Stir in cornstarch. Add to wok and cook, stirring, until the sauce thickens and gets shiny. Serve over rice.

1 serving: 150 Calories; 5 g Total Fat (1.5 g Mono, 3 g Poly, 0.5 g Sat); 25 mg Cholesterol; 10 g Carbohydrate (2 g Fibre, 3 g Sugar); 10 g Protein; 620 mg Sodium

Tip

To prepare the crab, place it in a saucepan and cover it with cold water. Bring the water to a simmer; remove the crab from the water and rinse under cold running water to stop the cooking process. To clean, turn the crab onto its back. Lift the triangular flap (the "apron"), then lift the spines underneath. Twist these spines off and discard. Hold the crab by the legs and pull off the shell. Remove and discard the gills on either side of the body, the jaw at the front and all the soft parts in the middle of the back; rinse well. Pull out and discard all the fat from the shell; rinse well. Split the cleaned body in half, and cut each half again between the legs. To crack the legs, stand each leg up on its narrow edge and hit each section with a sharpening steel or the blunt side of a knife.

Tabbouleh

Serves 4

Everyone recognizes parsley. For a long time, it was ubiquitous as a garnish on restaurant plates, either as whole leaves or finely minced and sprinkled over the whole plate. It seems like, for a while, we forgot that parsley had any flavour at all. If you grow parsley for cooking, plant a flat-leafed variety rather than the tasteless curly-leafed sort. Tabbouleh is known to most of us as a bulgur salad, accented with bits of tomato and parsley, but in its homeland, it is actually a salad of parsley, accented by bulgur and tomatoes. Try this version to see what you've been missing.

1/2 cup (125 mL) fine grind bulgur

2 cups (500 mL) finely chopped, fresh flat-leaf parsley (from about 4 cups lightly packed leaves)

1/2 cup (125 mL) finely chopped fresh mint

1/2 cup (125 mL) thinly sliced green onion

1 cup (250 mL) tomato, cut into 1/2 inch (12 mm) dice

6 Tbsp (90 mL) lemon juice

2 Tbsp (30 mL) extra virgin olive oil

1/2 tsp (2 mL) salt

1/4 tsp (1 mL) black pepper

2 small heads romaine lettuce, separated into individual leaves

Place bulgur in a small bowl; add cold water to cover and stir to combine. Set aside to soak until tender, about 20 minutes. Drain in a fine-mesh sieve, then transfer to a clean kitchen towel and wring out excess moisture. Transfer to a large bowl. Add parsley, mint, onion and tomato. Stir well.

Combine lemon juice, olive oil, salt and pepper in a small bowl. Whisk well. Stir into parsley mixture. Set aside at room temperature for 30 minutes to 1 hour to allow flavours to blend. Serve in a large bowl with romaine leaves for dipping, or heap a few spoonfuls of tabbouleh onto romaine leaves on individual plates.

1 serving: 220 Calories; 9 g Total Fat (6 g Mono, 1 g Poly, 1 g Sat); 0 mg Cholesterol; 33 g Carbohydrate (14 g Fibre, 6 g Sugar); 9 g Protein; 70 mg Sodium

Pinch parsley back to encourage bushy growth, and use the sprigs you pick off for eating. This plant can also be cut back regularly if you need a larger quantity in a recipe, and if not cut back too hard, it will sprout new growth.

Parsnip Breakfast Hash

Serves 4

Parsnips are an ideal vegetable for the Canadian climate—they aren't grown in warmer places because they need a frost or two to develop their full flavour. Unlike their more popular cousin, the carrot, parsnips are often ignored or disliked, but their herbal, even slightly floral, and nutty aroma and flavour adds complexity to any dish in which they're included. And perhaps that's the key: their aromatic qualities can be overpowering when parsnips are cooked on their own, but in combination with other ingredients, they're divine. Our breakfast hash uses a combination of parsnips and sweet potato where you would normally expect potato, for a more flavourful and more nutritious, yet still decadent, morning meal.

1 Tbsp (15 mL) grape seed oil

2 cups (500 mL) parsnips, cut into 1/2 inch (12 mm) dice

2 cups (500 mL) sweet potatoes, cut into 3/4 inch (2 cm) dice

1/2 lb (225 g) back bacon, cut into 1/2 inch (12 mm) dice

1 cup (250 mL) chopped red pepper

4 green onions, thinly sliced

1/4 cup (60 mL) chopped fresh oregano

salt and black pepper to taste

Heat oil in a large sauté pan over medium. Add parsnips and sweet potatoes. Cook, stirring occasionally, for about 5 minutes. Add back bacon. Cook, stirring occasionally, until veggies are tender and everything is starting to turn golden brown, about 5 minutes more. Add red pepper and green onion and cook, stirring occasionally, until peppers are tender-crisp, about 2 minutes. Add oregano, salt and pepper. Serve immediately.

1 serving: 230 Calories; 6 g Total Fat (1 g Mono, 2.5 g Poly, 1 g Sat); 35 mg Cholesterol; 33 g Carbohydrate (9 g Fibre, 8 g Sugar); 12 g Protein; 190 mg Sodium

The roots can be pulled up in autumn, after the first few frosts, and stored, like carrots, in damp sand in a cold, frost-free location. This plant can also be mulched with straw and pulled up in spring, before it sprouts new growth. Frost improves the flavour because some of the root starches are converted to sugar in freezing weather.

Pea and Ricotta Crostini

Serves 8 as an appetizer

There's something irresistible about peas fresh from the garden. Add to that the sudden hunger that often strikes as you're sitting on the back steps shelling, and unless you're careful to plant plenty, you might be lucky to see any peas make it from garden to dinner table. For those precious few that do survive the trip, why not show them off like the jewels they are in a simple, elegant dish that is both sweet and savoury all at once, and start your meal as you do a season in the garden—with peas.

1 1/2 cups (375 mL) shelled fresh peas

8 x 1/2 inch (12 mm) thick slices country-style bread, cut in half crosswise

8 cloves garlic, cut in half crosswise

15 oz (425 g) fresh ricotta cheese

Lemon Oil (see p. 33), as needed, for drizzling

salt and black pepper to taste

1/3 cup (75 mL) thinly sliced fresh basil

Bring a medium saucepan of salted water to a boil. Drop in peas and cook just until tender, about 1 1/2 minutes. Remove from heat and drain. Rinse under cold water until cool; drain well and set aside.

Preheat oven to 375°F (190°C). Arrange bread pieces in a single layer on a baking sheet. Toast until light golden, about 12 minutes. Pressing firmly, rub 1 side of each piece of bread with cut side of 1 garlic half. Top each piece of bread with 1 heaping Tbsp ricotta cheese, then peas, dividing equally. Press peas lightly into the cheese. Place 2 bread pieces on each of 8 plates. Drizzle lightly with lemon oil. Sprinkle with salt and pepper. Top with basil and serve.

1 serving: 190 Calories; 9 g Total Fat (3 g Mono, 0.5 g Poly, 4.5 g Sat); 25 mg Cholesterol; 18 g Carbohydrate (2 g Fibre, 2 g Sugar); 10 g Protein; 190 mg Sodium

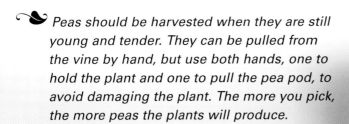 *Peas should be harvested when they are still young and tender. They can be pulled from the vine by hand, but use both hands, one to hold the plant and one to pull the pea pod, to avoid damaging the plant. The more you pick, the more peas the plants will produce.*

Three-pea Sauté with Tarragon

Serves 6

This recipe might just be the perfect spring side dish—delicious, beautifully green with a variety of shapes and textures, and quick to cook. Pea flowers are edible and taste much like pea shoots, with a mild, slightly nuttier pea flavour; if you're willing to sacrifice some future peas, they'll make this dish even prettier. But make sure you don't use sweet pea flowers— they're just as pretty, and look almost identical, but they are poisonous.

2 Tbsp (30 mL) butter

12 green onions, white parts only, thinly sliced

1 lb (454 g) snow peas, trimmed

1 cup (250 mL) fresh shelled peas, from about 1 lb (454 g) pods

1/4 lb (113 g) pea shoots, cut into 3 inch (7.5 cm) pieces

2 Tbsp (30 mL) fresh whole tarragon leaves

salt and black pepper to taste

Melt butter in a large sauté pan over medium heat. Add onions and cook, stirring, until they begin to soften, about 2 minutes. Add snow peas and shelled peas, and cook, stirring occasionally, until just tender, about 3 minutes. Add pea shoots, tarragon and salt and pepper. Stir just to coat and warm through. Serve immediately.

1 serving: 100 Calories; 4.5 g Total Fat (1 g Mono, 0 g Poly, 2.5 g Sat); 10 mg Cholesterol; 12 g Carbohydrate (3 g Fibre, 5 g Sugar); 5 g Protein; 65 mg Sodium

Peas are one of the most generous plants in the garden. They are one of a handful of plants that add nitrogen to the soil in which they are grown, enriching it for future crops. They can be eaten through almost the whole life cycle of the plant. Pea shoots are crunchy with just a hint of nuttiness; for cooked dishes, like this one, add them at the end, just to warm through, or use in salads and sandwiches. Pea vines (with or without flowers) are less tender; add them a little sooner to cooked dishes and let them cook until slightly wilted.

Roasted Red Pepper Jambalaya

Serves 4

Jamabalaya is a classic adaptation of Spanish paella. It can be separated into two major varieties. Creole, or red, jambalaya is cooked in a tomato sauce, and Cajun, or white, jambalaya is cooked with broth only. Ours is a red version, but we've replaced the tomato sauce with a purée of roasted red peppers to add smoky, complex flavour to the dish.

4 red peppers

5 tsp (25 mL) grape seed oil, *divided*

1/2 lb (225 g) andouille or chorizo sausage, sliced 1/2 inch (12 mm) thick

2 boneless, skinless chicken breasts, cut into bite-sized pieces

2 stalks celery, chopped

1 green pepper, chopped

1 small onion, chopped

3 cloves garlic, minced

1/2 tsp (2 mL) dried oregano

1/2 tsp (2 mL) dried thyme

1/2 tsp (2 mL) paprika

1/4 tsp (1 mL) cayenne

1 tsp (5 mL) coarse salt

1/4 tsp (1 mL) black pepper

(see next page)

Preheat grill to medium-high or oven to 425°F (220°C). Rub red peppers lightly with 1 tsp (5 mL) oil. Arrange in a single layer on the grill or a baking sheet. Cook, turning occasionally, until peppers collapse and skin is blackened and bubbling on all sides, 7 to 10 minutes. Transfer to heat-proof bowl and cover with plastic wrap. Set aside for about 10 minutes.

Peel or rub off the skins, then pull out and discard the cores and as many of the seeds as possible. Transfer pepper flesh to a blender (or use a clean bowl and a hand blender) and purée until smooth, adding as much of the juices from the bowl as necessary to get the blender moving. You should have about 1 cup (250 mL) pepper purée. Set aside.

Heat a large saucepan over medium-low. Add sausage slices and cook until they start to give off some of their oil, about 3 to 4 minutes. Increase the heat to medium and cook until lightly browned. Remove from pan with a slotted spoon and set aside.

Add 2 tsp (10 mL) oil to the pan. Add chicken and cook until golden on all sides, about 4 minutes. Remove from the pan with a slotted spoon and add to sausage slices.

Add remaining 2 tsp (10 mL) oil to the saucepan. Cook celery, green pepper, onion, garlic, oregano, thyme, paprika, cayenne, salt and pepper, stirring and scraping any browned bits from the bottom of the pan with a wooden spoon, until onion has softened, about 4 minutes. Add rice and cook, stirring, until coated with oil, about 2 minutes.

Add roasted pepper purée, sausage, chicken, chicken broth and water. Stir and bring to a boil. Reduce heat to medium-low, cover and simmer until rice is almost tender, about 15 minutes. Add prawns and cook, stirring occasionally, until prawns are cooked through, 4 to 5 minutes. Taste and adjust seasoning with salt, pepper and hot pepper sauce. Divide among 4 bowls, sprinkle with parsley and serve immediately with additional hot sauce on the side.

1 serving: 670 Calories; 26 g Total Fat (2 g Mono, 5 g Poly, 7 g Sat); 195 mg Cholesterol; 52 g Carbohydrate; 5 g Fibre, 7 g Sugar); 23 g Protein; 350 mg Sodium

1 cup (250 mL) white long grain rice

1 cup (250 mL) chicken broth

1 cup (250 mL) water

1/2 lb (225 g) prawns, peeled and deveined

hot pepper sauce to taste

1/4 cup (60 mL) finely chopped fresh parsley

Chicken Panini with Honey Balsamic Glazed Peppers and Lemon Aïoli

Serves 4

At first glance, this chicken sandwich looks like a lot of work, but with its delicious balsamic and honey glazed peppers and onions, it is well worth the effort. After all, if this were just any chicken sandwich, you wouldn't need a recipe, would you? Pair it with soup or a salad for dinner. For a more authentic panini (and one that holds together better), cover two bricks in aluminum foil to place on top of the sandwiches while they grill.

2 Tbsp (15 mL) grape seed oil, *divided*

juice and finely grated zest of 1 lemon

2 cloves garlic, minced

pinch *each* of salt and black pepper

2 boneless, skinless chicken breasts

1/2 medium red onion, thinly sliced lengthwise

2 medium bell peppers, any colour but green, halved, seeded and sliced crosswise 1/2 inch (12 mm) thick

1 Tbsp (15 mL) honey

1 Tbsp (15 mL) balsamic vinegar

1 piece foccacia, cut into quarters

1/2 cup (125 mL) Lemon Aïoli (see opposite)

8 oz (225 g) sliced fontina cheese

2 cups (500 mL) baby spinach leaves

Combine 1 Tbsp (15 mL) oil, lemon juice and zest, garlic, salt and pepper in a shallow dish. Mix well. Carefully cut chicken breasts in half horizontally and add to marinade. Turn to coat, then cover and refrigerate 30 minutes.

Heat remaining 1 Tbsp (15 mL) oil in a medium sauté pan over medium. Add onions and cook, stirring occasionally, until softened and golden brown, about 10 minutes. Add peppers, honey and balsamic vinegar. Reduce heat to low and cook, stirring occasionally, until liquid has mostly all evaporated, about 5 minutes more. Remove from heat and set aside. Can be prepared ahead; store in an airtight container in the refrigerator up to 4 days.

Preheat grill to medium. Grill chicken, flipping once, until cooked through, 4 to 5 minutes. Remove from heat and set aside.

Split bread in half horizontally. Spread some aïoli on each piece, then top with cheese slices. Divide peppers and onions among the 4 sandwiches, piling them onto one piece of the bread, then repeat with spinach and top with 1 piece of chicken breast. Close sandwiches and flatten firmly with a foil-covered brick or a plate. Grill, topped with 2 foil-covered bricks if possible (each brick should cover 2 sandwiches), until bread is crusty and cheese melts, 3 to 4 minutes on each side.

1 sandwich: 830 Calories; 38 g Total Fat (5 g Mono, 6 g Poly, 11 g Sat); 145 mg Cholesterol; 62 g Carbohydrate (5 g Fibre, 9 g Sugar); 53 g Protein; 1160 mg Sodium

Lemon Aïoli

2 cloves garlic

1 tsp (5 mL) lemon zest

1/4 tsp (1 mL) salt

1 egg yolk

black pepper to taste

1/2 cup (125 mL) extra virgin olive oil

1 Tbsp (15 mL) lemon juice

Grind garlic and salt into a smooth paste in a mortar (or mash with the side of a knife on a cutting board). Transfer to a mixing bowl. Add egg yolk and pepper. Beat with a whisk until the mixture turns pale yellow. Drizzle in oil, whisking constantly. Whisk in lemon juice. Taste and adjust seasoning with additional salt and lemon juice. Can be prepared 1 day ahead; store, covered, in the refrigerator.

2 Tbsp (30 mL): 90 Calories; 10 g Total Fat (7 g Mono, 1 g Poly, 1.5 g Sat); 35 mg Cholesterol; trace Carbohydrate; 0 g Fibre, 0 g Sugar); 1 g Protein; 100 mg Sodium

Grilled Pork Tenderloin with Salsa Verde

Serves 4

Hot peppers can be difficult to grow in Canada; often they don't reach their full intensity because of our short season. But the beautiful kaleidoscope of colours of hot peppers, from tiny elongated ones, to plump cherry peppers, to the larger semi-hot banana peppers, is unmatched. Luckily, a little chili goes a long way, as you'll see in the this fiery sauce. Using chilies of a colour other than green will muddy the colour of the sauce a little.

Salsa Verde

3 cloves garlic, unpeeled

1 lb (454 g) fresh tomatillos, husked

1 small onion, cut vertically into quarters

6 serrano chilies or 4 jalapeño chilies

1/2 cup (125 mL) chopped fresh cilantro

1/4 cup (60 mL) chopped fresh mint

1/4 cup (60 mL) chopped fresh parsley

1/2 tsp (2 mL) sugar, or more to taste

coarse salt to taste

2 Tbsp (30 mL) grape seed oil

1/4 tsp (1 mL) ground cumin

1 cup (250 mL) chicken broth

2 Tbsp (30 mL) fresh lime juice, or more to taste

Preheat barbecue to medium-high. Thread garlic cloves onto a pre-soaked bamboo skewer to make grilling them easier. Rinse tomatillos to get rid of stickiness on the skin. Place garlic, tomatillos, onion and chilies on lightly greased grill and cook, turning occasionally, until dark brown blisters form on all sides. Remove small items first: garlic and chilies will take about 4 minutes, tomatillos 6 minutes and onion 9 minutes. Set aside to cool.

Once cool, peel garlic. Cut off and discard core from onion pieces. Scrape burnt skin from chilies and stem them. If you want a hot salsa, leave seeds in the chilies; if you prefer it a little milder, scrape out and discard most of the seeds. Chop garlic, onion and chilies, and transfer to a blender. Add tomatillos, cilantro, mint, parsley and sugar. Purée until smooth. Season with coarse salt.

Heat oil in a large saucepan over high. Add tomatillo mixture and cumin. Cook, stirring, until slightly thickened, about 2 minutes. Add chicken broth and lime juice. Bring to a boil, then reduce heat to medium and simmer until reduced to about 2 1/2 cups (625 mL), about 10 minutes. Adjust seasoning, if necessary. Cool to room temperature, then cover and store in refrigerator up to 5 days or in freezer up to 2 months.

1/2 cup (125 mL): 130 Calories; 8 g Total Fat (1.5 g Mono, 6 g Poly, 0.5 g Sat); 0 mg Cholesterol; 13 g Carbohydrate (4 g Fibre, 7 g Sugar); 2 g Protein; 150 mg Sodium

Grilled Pork Tenderloin

1 lb (454 g) pork tenderloin

2 tsp (10 mL) grape seed oil

1/4 tsp (1 mL) salt

1/4 tsp (1 mL) black pepper

1/2 tsp (2 mL) crushed cumin seeds

Preheat grill to medium-high. Rub the pork lightly with oil, then sprinkle all over with salt, pepper and cumin. Grill with lid closed, turning once about halfway through cooking time, until an instant-read thermometer reads 145°F (63°C), about 20 minutes. Transfer pork to a plate, tent loosely with foil and set aside to rest for 5 minutes.

Slice pork on the diagonal into 1/2 inch (12 mm) thick medallions. To serve, fan medallions on 4 plates or a serving platter and drizzle with salsa verde. Serve mellow sides, such as mildly seasoned rice or potatoes to counter some of the heat.

1 serving: 300 Calories; 17 g Total Fat (4.5 g Mono, 8 g Poly, 3 g Sat); 75 mg Cholesterol; 13 g Carbohydrate (4 g Fibre, 7 g Sugar); 25 g Protein; 350 mg Sodium

Tip

Any type of chili pepper will work in this recipe—just be aware of how much heat you're adding and adjust the number of chilies used according to your tolerance for heat.

New Potatoes with Roasted Garlic, Lemon and Dill

Serves 4

New potatoes just might be the best reason to grow your own potatoes. I could happily pick them all at this stage—no need for peeling or chopping, and their flesh is creamy smooth and delicately flavoured. At planting time, look for the Yukon Gold variety developed in Canada, which, like other varieties with yellow, red or purple flesh, are fuller flavoured than white-fleshed varieties. Tossed in a creamy, lightly flavoured yogurt dressing, these potatoes make a great side dish for hearty meat dishes like our Yogurt-marinated Lamb (p. 88) when served hot (along with another vegetable, of course), or eat at room temperature for a tangy alternative to traditional potato salad.

1/2 cup (125 mL) plain Balkan-style yogurt

juice and finely grated zest from 1 lemon

1/2 bunch of fresh dill, chopped

salt and black pepper to taste

2 heads roasted garlic (see p. 73)

2 lbs (900 g) new potatoes

Combine yogurt, lemon juice and zest, dill, salt and pepper in a small bowl or the bowl of a blender. Mix well. Squeeze in roasted garlic cloves, discarding papery husks. Purée the mixture with a blender (or hand blender) until smooth. Mixture can be made ahead and kept in an airtight container in the refrigerator overnight; the flavours will intensify.

Scrub potatoes and cut in halves or quarters if they are large. Transfer to a medium saucepan and cover with cold water. Bring to a boil, then reduce heat and simmer until tender, about 10 minutes. Drain well. Toss with yogurt mixture and serve immediately.

1 serving: 320 Calories; 10 g Total Fat (4.5 g Mono, 1 g Poly, 3 g Sat); 5 mg Cholesterol; 50 g Carbohydrate (3 g Fibre, 2 g Sugar); 8 g Protein; 35 mg Sodium

The tubers begin to form around the same time the plants begin to flower, usually in August. You can dig up a few tubers at a time from this point on as you need them. The remaining crop should be dug up in autumn once the plants have withered, but before the first hard frost. Let them dry for a few hours on the soil, and then brush the dirt off and store the tubers in a cold, dark place. You can even save a few of the smaller tubers for planting the following spring.

114

Salt-roasted Potatoes

Serves 4

Salt roasting is a traditional cooking method that brings out the full flavour of whatever you cook in this way, making it taste more like itself. Here, you'll get the full earthy and mineral flavour of the potatoes, along with hints of the rosemary sprinkled in the salt. Don't worry, they won't taste salty; the salt doesn't penetrate beyond the skin of the potatoes. Once you've tried it, you'll find it worth experimenting with this technique. Fish, especially, cooks to perfection in salt, retaining its moisture while cooking all the way through. Make sure whatever you cook this way is top quality, though, because flavours are concentrated.

2 cloves garlic, halved

extra virgin olive oil, as needed

2 lbs (900 g) potatoes, scrubbed but not peeled, cut up if large (but beware, the cut edges will absorb more salt)

1 1/2 lbs (680 g) coarse kosher salt

1/4 cup (60 mL) flour

2 Tbsp (30 mL) fresh rosemary, roughly chopped

1/2 cup (125 mL) water

Preheat oven to 450°F (230°C). Pressing firmly, rub cut ends of garlic on the bottom and sides of a 12 inch (30 cm) gratin dish. Brush lightly with oil. Arrange the potatoes in a single layer in the dish.

In a large bowl, combine salt, flour and rosemary. Mix well. Add water gradually, stirring until thoroughly combined. Pour over potatoes, filling in any gaps between them. The salt mixture should cover the potatoes completely. Roast for 1 hour and 15 minutes. Remove from the oven. Set aside to cool slightly, about 5 minutes. Invert onto a serving platter. Drizzle with olive oil. To serve, break the salt and pull the potatoes out with tongs.

1 serving: 240 Calories; 4 g Total Fat (3 g Mono, 0 g Poly, 0.5 g Sat); 0 mg Cholesterol; 46 g Carbohydrate (4 g Fibre, 2 g Sugar); 6 g Protein; 340 mg Sodium

All parts of the potato plant are poisonous except the tubers, and they can become poisonous if they are exposed to light. Green flesh is a good indication that your potatoes have been exposed to light. To protect your potatoes, mound soil around the plants, 1 inch (2.5 cm) or so per week, from midsummer to autumn. A straw mulch also effectively shades the developing tubers.

Radish, Cucumber and Grilled Spring Onions

Serves 4

Crisp, juicy and mildly peppery, radishes are harbingers of spring. Planted early, they offer quick rewards for Canadian gardeners and gourmands alike—they taste best when grown in cool weather and picked young. Their peppery bite wakes the palate from the sweet root vegetables of winter and whets the appetite for the meal to come. If you are a radish lover, don't ignore the Asian varieties, including the large white daikons, the green-skinned varieties and the beautiful red-fleshed radishes sometimes called watermelon radishes.

clove garlic, minced

tsp (2 mL) salt

1 Tbsp (15 mL) grainy Dijon mustard

1 Tbsp (15 mL) red wine vinegar

1/4 tsp (1 mL) black pepper

1/4 cup (60 mL) extra virgin olive oil, plus more as needed, for drizzling

12 green or spring onions

1/2 seedless cucumber

1 to 2 small heads butter lettuce, chopped

16 smallish radishes, trimmed

1 handful of whole mint leaves

For the dressing, mash garlic and salt with the side of your knife to form a paste. Transfer to a medium bowl and add mustard, vinegar and pepper. Whisk thoroughly. Slowly add oil, whisking constantly, until emulsified. If you prefer a slightly thicker dressing, use a hand blender rather than a whisk to emulsify the dressing.

Trim any wilted parts from the onions. Heat a large dry sauté pan over medium-high. Add onions and cook until golden, about 30 seconds to 1 minute on each side. Drizzle oil over top and sprinkle with salt. Set aside.

Cut cucumber in half lengthwise, then slice about 1/4 inch (6 mm) thick. Combine in a large bowl with lettuce, radishes and mint. Drizzle with vinaigrette and toss to coat. Divide among 4 plates. Lay onions over top and serve immediately.

1 serving: 100 Calories; 4.5 g Total Fat (3 g Mono, 0.5 g Poly, 0.5 g Sat); 0 mg Cholesterol; 13 g Carbohydrate (7 g Fibre, 5 g Sugar); 4 g Protein; 35 mg Sodium

Spring radishes should be picked and eaten as soon as the roots develop. The flavour and texture deteriorates quickly if they are left in the ground or stored for too long. Daikon and Spanish radishes are usually started in summer to be ready for harvest in late autumn. They can be stored like carrots, in moist sand in a cool, dry location. They can also be pickled.

Raspberry Sponge Cake

Serves 10 to 12

Whether cultivated carefully in your garden or running wild in a corner of the yard or over the fence in the alley, raspberries at their peak taste like a burst of summer sunshine on the tongue. Part of their appeal may be the danger inherent in picking them; I have distinct memories of coming home from picking raspberries as a child, my arms so scratched up from the thorns that they were nearly the colour of the raspberries themselves. If you're looking for a new way to enjoy your raspberries, try this feather-light pink cake perfumed and coloured with fresh raspberry purée and served with a few more fresh berries on the side.

1 1/2 cups (375 mL) fresh raspberries

2 cups (550 mL) cake flour

1 1/2 cups (375 mL) plus 2 Tbsp (37 mL) sugar, *divided*

2 tsp (10 mL) baking powder

1/2 tsp (2 mL) salt

1/2 cup (125 mL) grape seed oil

7 egg yolks

zest from 1 lemon

1 tsp (5 mL) vanilla

10 egg whites

1 1/4 tsp (6 mL) cream of tartar

Place raspberries in a blender and purée until smooth. Press through a fine-mesh sieve and discard seeds. Set aside.

Preheat oven to 325°F (160°C). Combine flour, 1 1/4 cup (300 mL) plus 2 1/2 Tbsp (37 mL) sugar, baking powder and salt in a large mixing bowl. Beat for 1 minute. Add oil, egg yolks, raspberry purée, lemon zest and vanilla and beat until smooth, about 1 minute.

In the bowl of a mixer or a second large mixing bowl, beat egg whites until frothy. Add cream of tartar and beat to soft peaks. Add 2 Tbsp (30 mL) sugar and beat to stiff peaks. Carefully fold egg white mixture into batter with a balloon whisk just until incorporated. Pour into an ungreased 10 inch (25 cm) tube pan, then run a butter knife through the batter to pop any air pockets. Sprinkle the remaining 2 Tbsp (30 mL) sugar over top. Bake until a skewer inserted in the centre comes out clean, about 55 minutes. Remove from the oven and invert the pan over the neck of a wine bottle or a shot glass (to prevent the cake from deflating as it cools), and cool the cake completely in the pan, about 1 1/2 hours.

Run a knife inside the edges of the pan to loosen the cake and remove the outside of the pan. Run the knife under the bottom of the cake to loosen. Invert onto a greased wire rack and re-invert onto a serving plate. Serve with whipped cream or ice cream and fresh raspberries on the side.

1 serving: 330 Calories; 14 g Total Fat (3.5 g Mono, 8 g Poly, 2 g Sat); 135 mg Cholesterol; 42 g Carbohydrate (2 g Fibre, 4 g Sugar); 9 g Protein; 220 mg Sodium

Pick the berries as soon as they are ripe, in mid- to late summer. All the fruit does not ripen at once, and you can harvest it for a month or more. Some raspberry varieties are ever-bearing and produce fruit in flushes from mid-summer through autumn.

Rhubarb Custard Tarts

Serves 4

When you grow rhubarb, it becomes much like zucchini—you're always looking for ways to use it up. But once you try this recipe, you may suddenly find yourself wishing you had more. Tart rhubarb and creamy, sweet custard are a perfect combination, but when the two sit atop a crisp, flaky pastry crust, they are even more delicious. Rhubarb is so good that we've even provided another recipe for it (see opposite).

5 stalks rhubarb, cut in 4 inch (10 cm) pieces

2 Tbsp (30 mL) sugar

3 Tbsp (45 mL) water

1 1/4 cups (300 mL) milk

2/3 cup (150 mL) whipping cream

1 vanilla bean, split

6 egg yolks, *divided*

6 Tbsp (90 mL) superfine sugar

2 Tbsp (30 mL) flour

1 package frozen puff pastry, thawed

1 Tbsp (15 mL) chopped blanched almonds

confectioner's sugar, for dusting

Lay rhubarb in a single layer in a wide saucepan. Sprinkle sugar over top and add water. Bring to a simmer over medium, then gently turn over rhubarb pieces, turn off the heat and cover. Set aside to cool to room temperature.

In a medium saucepan, combine milk and cream. Scrape in seeds from vanilla bean and add the pod. Bring to a boil, then remove from heat.

In a medium bowl, combine 5 egg yolks, sugar and flour. Whisk until well combined. Pull vanilla bean pod from hot milk and discard. Slowly pour hot milk, a little at a time, into egg yolk mixture, whisking constantly. Pour mixture back into the milk saucepan and set over low heat. Cook, whisking constantly, until thick enough to coat the back of a spoon, about 5 minutes, being careful not to let it boil.

Preheat oven to 400°F (200°C). Roll out puff pastry to 1/4 inch (6 mm). Cut into 5 inch (12.5 cm) squares. Spread custard over the top of each one, leaving a 1/4 inch (6 mm) border uncovered. Top with rhubarb pieces, sprinkle almonds over and gently push them into the custard. Brush tops with remaining egg yolk. Dust with confectioner's sugar. Bake until puffed and golden, about 20 minutes.

Remove from oven and cool slightly, about 5 to 10 minutes. Dust with additional confectioner's sugar and serve warm.

1 serving: *870 Calories; 54 g Total Fat (27 g Mono, 7 g Poly, 17 g Sat); 345 mg Cholesterol; 82 g Carbohydrate; 3 g Fibre, 32 g Sugar); 17 g Protein; 320 mg Sodium*

Vanilla-rose Rhubarb Compote

Makes about 5 cups (1.25 L)

Serve this compote warm or cold as an accompaniment to cakes, layered with yogurt and granola or over ice cream. Rose water is available at Middle Eastern or specialty grocers.

1 1/2 cups (375 mL) sugar

2 cups (500 mL) water

1 lb (454 g) rhubarb, cut diagonally into 1/4 inch (6 mm) thick slices (about 2 cups, 500 mL)

1/2 tsp (2 mL) rose water

1/4 tsp (1 mL) vanilla

Combine sugar and water in a large saucepan. Bring to a simmer and cook, stirring, until sugar is dissolved. Add rhubarb. Return to a simmer, then remove pan from heat. Gently stir in rose water and vanilla, being careful not to break up the rhubarb. Set aside to cool, stirring occasionally. Cover and chill until ready to use. Refrigerate up to 5 days, or freeze up to 3 months.

1/2 cup (125 mL): 15 Calories; 0 g Total Fat (0 g Mono, 0 g Poly, 0 g Sat); 0 mg Cholesterol; 4 g Carbohydrate (trace Fibre, 2 g Sugar); 0 g Protein; 0 mg Sodium

Rhubarb Shortbread Bars

Makes 24 bars

Beware: these rhubarb shortbread squares are irresistible. The combination of tart rhubarb and buttery shortbread just might be perfection. Serve at room temperature, or freeze and eat them straight from the freezer for a cool treat. You won't need more than one bite to send you out to the nursery for more rhubarb plants for your garden.

1 lb (454 g) rhubarb, cut into 1 inch (2.5 cm) pieces

3 cups (750 mL) sugar, *divided*

1/2 cup (125 mL) water

1 vanilla bean, split

4 cups (1 L) flour

2 tsp (10 mL) baking powder

1/4 tsp (1 mL) salt

1 lb (454 g) butter

4 egg yolks

confectioner's sugar, for dusting

Combine rhubarb, 1 cup (250 mL) sugar and water in a small saucepan. Scrape the seeds from the vanilla bean into the pot and reserve the pod for another use. Cook over medium heat, stirring occasionally, until rhubarb falls apart and thickens, about 10 minutes. Set aside to cool completely.

Sift together flour, baking powder and salt in a medium bowl. Mix well and set aside. In the bowl of a mixer or a large bowl, cream together butter and remaining 2 cups (500 mL) sugar until light and fluffy. Add egg yolks and beat until smooth. Slowly add dry ingredients, beating constantly, and mix until just incorporated. Divide dough into 2 equal portions and form into balls. Wrap tightly in plastic wrap and refrigerate at least 1 hour.

Preheat oven to 350°F (175°C). Grate one ball of dough into the bottom of a greased 9 x 13 inch (23 x 33 cm) baking dish to form an even layer across the bottom. Do not pat. Spread rhubarb mixture over the dough. Grate second ball of dough over rhubarb. Pat lightly. Bake until golden on top, about 40 minutes. Dust generously with confectioner's sugar. Cool completely in pan on a wire rack, then chill at least 3 minutes before cutting into bars. Keep in an airtight container at room temperature up to 4 days or freeze up to 3 months.

1 bar: 320 Calories; 16 g Total Fat (4.5 g Mono, 1 g Poly, 10 g Sat); 75 mg Cholesterol; 41 g Carbohydrate (trace Fibre, 25 g Sugar); 3 g Protein; 160 mg Sodium

Harvest rhubarb stems by pulling them firmly and cleanly from the base of the plant. The leaves can then be cut from the stems with a sharp knife and composted or spread around the base of the plant to conserve moisture, suppress weed growth and return nutrients to the soil. Don't remove more than half the stems from the plant in one year. Rhubarb's flavour is better earlier in summer, and harvesting generally stops by early July when the stems start to become dry, pithy and bitter.

Rosemary Grilled Chicken with Gremolata

Serves 4

Though rosemary's Latin name means "dew of the sea," with its slightly astringent, piney scent and flavour, it evokes damp, fragrant woods more than the salty sea air. It can be difficult to grow in the garden alongside other plants because it prefers well-drained, slightly less fertile than average soil. But it's well worth dedicating a pot or two to rosemary, or pair it with other like-minded herbs such as lavender. Its outdoorsy flavour works particularly well with grilled chicken, pork or lamb. Remarkably, it has a distinct mustard-like scent when burned, so we've played that up by pairing it with grainy Dijon mustard in this recipe.

2 Tbsp (30 mL) grainy Dijon mustard

1/4 cup (60 mL) chopped fresh rosemary

1/4 cup (60 mL) lemon juice

1 Tbsp (15 mL) brown sugar

3 Tbsp (45 mL) extra virgin olive oil

4 cloves garlic, minced

1/2 tsp (2 mL) *each* salt and black pepper

4 boneless, skinless chicken breasts

Combine all ingredients except the chicken in a large bowl. Stir until thoroughly combined. Add chicken and toss until coated. Cover and refrigerate about 2 hours, turning once or twice.

Preheat grill to medium-high. Grill the chicken with the lid closed until just cooked through, about 7 minutes on each side. Serve topped with Rosemary Gremolata (see opposite).

1 serving: 380 Calories; 14 g Total Fat (9 g Mono, 1.5 g Poly, 2.5 g Sat); 135 mg Cholesterol; 8 g Carbohydrate (0 g Fibre, 4 g Sugar); 55 g Protein; 250 mg Sodium

Combine all ingredients in a small bowl and mix thoroughly.

1/4 cup (60 mL): *20 Calories; 0 g Total Fat (0 g Mono, 0 g Poly, 0 g Sat); 0 mg Cholesterol; 4 g Carbohydrates (1 g Fibre, 0 g Sugar); trace Protein; 250 mg Sodium*

Rosemary Gremolata

1/4 cup (60 mL) chopped flat-leaf parsley

zest from 1 lemon

2 cloves garlic, minced

1 tsp (5 mL) finely chopped fresh rosemary

pinch *each* of salt and black pepper

Rutabaga and Daikon Sprout Salad

Serves 4

Rutabaga (also called swede and neep) is an oft-maligned vegetable. But how many of those who say they dislike it know what it tastes like, or even what it looks like? Perhaps it would be better termed a lost or forgotten vegetable. In grocery stores, you'll find rutabagas and turnips confused as often as you will sweet potatoes and yams. While it's true that rutabagas and turnips can be used in the same ways, rutabagas are milder tasting and sweeter, especially if harvested after a frost, and you can easily recognize them by their yellower colour. Like many other root veggies, rutabagas are delicious as a mash, in a stew or soup and especially roasted, where the outsides caramelize into golden sweetness—try cutting them into French fry shapes and roasting with olive oil and salt. But they're equally as delicious in this simple salad, where they're paire with peppery daikon radish sprouts and Miso Ginger Dressing.

3 cups (750 mL) peeled, julienned rutabaga

1 cup (250 mL) daikon sprouts

1/4 cup (60 mL) thinly sliced green onion

Miso Ginger Dressing (see opposite)

If the rutabagas you julienned were small, use them raw. If they were large, or if you prefer a milder flavour, bring a medium saucepan of salted water to a boil, add the rutabaga and cook for 1 minute. Drain and refresh in ice water. Drain well again before adding to salad.

Combine rutabaga, daikon sprouts and green onion in a large bowl. Drizzle about 1/4 cup (60 mL) dressing over and toss to coat. Divide among 4 serving plates and serve immediately.

1 serving: 120 Calories; 4.5 g Total Fat (1 g Mono, 3 g Poly, 0 g Sat); 0 mg Cholesterol; 17 g Carbohydrate; 3 g Fibre, 8 g Sugar); 4 g Protein; 130 mg Sodium

Place vinegar, miso paste, pickled ginger, brown sugar and soy sauce in a blender and purée until smooth. With the blender still running, slowly drizzle in both oils and blend until emulsified.

1/4 cup (60 mL): 190 Calories; 16 g Total Fat (4 g Mono, 11 g Poly, 1.5 g Sat); 0 mg Cholesterol; 10 g Carbohydrate (trace Fibre, 11 g Sugar); 1 g Protein; 420 mg Sodium

Rutabaga can be used as soon as the root is plump and round, but can also be left in the ground so the first few autumn frosts can sweeten the roots.

Miso Ginger Dressing

1/3 cup (75 mL) rice vinegar

2 Tbsp (30 mL) white or yellow miso paste

2 Tbsp (30 mL) minced pickled ginger

1 Tbsp (15 mL) brown sugar

1 Tbsp (15 mL) light soy sauce

1/4 cup (60 mL) peanut oil or grape seed oil

2 tsp (10 mL) sesame oil

Sage-brined Fried Chicken

Serves 4

Sage's grey-green, suede-like leaves add beauty and romance to the garden. Its warm, fragrant, slightly nutty flavour is a classic with pork and poultry, in stuffings and in a browned butter sauce over pasta. But sage's intense flavour can be overpowering if you are heavy-handed with it. Here, we used it in a milk and yogurt brine to infuse chicken with delicate herbal flavour. Sage appears subtly again in the honey drizzled over the finished fried chicken, a delicious pairing passed down from my grandmother. If you've never tried fried chicken with honey, you absolutely must. Trust me, you'll thank my gramma after the first bite.

2 3/4 cups (675 mL) milk, *divided* (or more if necessary)

1/4 cup (60 mL) salt

1/2 cup (125 mL) coarsely chopped sage

3/4 cup (175 mL) yogurt

1 whole frying chicken

1 cup (250 mL) flour

1 tsp (5 mL) salt

1 Tbsp (15 mL) black pepper

vegetable oil, as needed, for frying

In a small saucepan, bring 3/4 cup (175 mL) milk to a boil. Remove from heat and add salt, stirring until dissolved. Add sage. Set aside to cool to room temperature. Stir in yogurt and remaining 2 cups (500 mL) milk. Transfer to a shallow dish.

With poultry shears or a sharp knife, begin at the tail end of the chicken and cut along one side of the backbone and then the other to remove it. Then, with the chicken breast side down, use a sharp knife to cut through the keel bone in the centre of the breast, splitting the chicken in half. Cut between the breast and leg portions of each half to quarter the chicken. Then cut through the joint on each leg piece, separating the drumstick from the thigh. Finally, cut the wings from the breast. If you prefer more evenly sized pieces, you may wish to cut each breast crosswise into 2 or 3 pieces. Add chicken pieces in a single layer to the brine. If necessary, add more milk so that chicken is covered. Cover and refrigerate overnight.

Drain off and discard brine. Combine flour, salt and pepper on a plate (a pie plate also works well). Mix well. Dredge chicken pieces in flour to coat, then set aside for a few minutes while you heat the oil.

Place 1/2 inch (12 mm) oil in a large, heavy sauté pan over medium-high. Test the oil with a little flour: the flour should sizzle when it hits the oil (or if you have a deep-fat/candy thermometer, it should register 350°F, 175°C). Add the chicken to the pan skin side down in a single layer. Cook until skin is lightly browned, about 3 minutes, then carefully turn the pieces over. Cook on the second side until slightly more brown than the first, 3 to 4 minutes more. Reduce heat to medium and turn over again to cook a few minutes more. Continue cooking over medium heat, turning every 3 or 4 minutes, until the chicken is well browned and an instant-read thermometer registers 170°F (77°C). Smaller pieces such as the wings will cook faster and will need to be removed sooner than others. Use a slotted spoon to remove the chicken pieces and transfer them to paper towels to drain. Serve warm or cold with sage-infused honey on the side for drizzling.

1 serving: 600 Calories; 20 g Total Fat (10 g Mono, 4.5 g Poly, 3 g Sat); 120 mg Cholesterol; 66 g Carbohydrate (4 g Fibre, 35 g Sugar); 41 g Protein; 1930 mg Sodium

Sage-infused Honey

1 cup (250 mL) honey

1/4 cup (60 mL) lightly packed fresh sage leaves

Heat honey in a small saucepan over medium-high. Stir in sage leaves and set aside to cool to room temperature. Once cool, pour through a fine-mesh sieve and discard sage leaves.

2 Tbsp (30 mL): 130 Calories; 0 g Total Fat (0 g Mono, 0 g Poly, 0 g Sat); 0 mg Cholesterol; 36 g Carbohydrate (1 g Fibre, 32 g Sugar); 0 g Protein; 0 mg Sodium

Prawns with Sorrel and Asparagus

Serves 4

Sorrel is an adaptable, easy-going plant. If you want it in your garden, plant it. It's happy to oblige by being fairly undemanding of water, light, soil conditions, etc. If you don't want it in your garden...well, it's probably there anyway, in one form or another, growing as a weed. The upside is that it offers a delectable reward for weeding, adding a bright, lemony flavour to whatever dish it goes into. The different varieties of sorrel are interchangeable in any recipe, but cultivated varieties must be cut into strips to keep them from being tough, whereas wild sorrel, especially if the leaves are small, can be used as whole leaves.

3 Tbsp (45 mL) butter

2 cloves garlic, minced

3 cups (750 mL) lightly packed sorrel, cut crosswise into 1/2 inch (12 mm) strips

2 bunches of asparagus, trimmed and cut into 1 inch (3.8 cm) pieces

1 1/2 lbs (680 g) prawns, peeled and deveined

1/2 cup (125 mL) water

1 tsp (5 mL) salt

black pepper to taste

Melt butter in a large, non-stick sauté pan over medium-low heat. Add garlic and cook, stirring, until fragrant, about 1 minute. Add sorrel. Cook, stirring occasionally, until wilted, about 2 minutes. Increase heat to medium. Add asparagus and prawns. Cook, stirring, until shrimp begin to colour, about 2 minutes. Add water and cover. Cook for 5 minutes, stirring halfway through. Season with salt and pepper. Serve over rice or other grain.

1 serving: 280 Calories; 12 g Total Fat (2.5 g Mono, 1.5 g Poly, 0 g Sat); 280 mg Cholesterol; 7 g Carbohydrate (3 g Fibre, 2 g Sugar); 37 g Protein; 910 mg Sodium

Tip

Do not use an aluminum pan to cook this recipe because sorrel reacts chemically with aluminum and will both look and taste terrible.

Pick leaves as needed in spring and early summer. Remove flower spikes as they emerge to prolong the leaf harvest. Once the weather warms up and the plant goes to flower, the leaves lose their pleasant flavour. If you cut the plant back a bit at this point, you will have fresh leaves to harvest in late summer and autumn when the weather cools again.

Spanakopita

Makes 24 triangles

Spinach has gained many fans since we learned not to overcook it. Heated in a pan with a little oil or butter just until it wilts, it's divine, and the young leaves are a favourite green for salads. But there is something to be said for spinach cooked until velvety smooth, especially with something crisp to contrast with it. Spanakopita has become a favourite appetizer in Greek restaurants and beyond, but in Greece, it is most often eaten as a snack on the run or between meals rather than as part of a meal. It's a relatively easy pastry to make, once you get the hang of working with phyllo, and homemade tastes much better than the frozen store-bought versions. Whether on its own as a snack, as an appetizer, or 2 or 3 with a salad as a full meal, spanakopita is proof that spinach and feta are made for one another.

4 cups (500 mL) lightly packed, chopped fresh spinach

2 tsp (10 mL) olive oil

4 cloves garlic, minced

6 green onions, chopped

1/4 cup (60 mL) chopped fresh dill

2 Tbsp (30 mL) chopped fresh oregano

1/2 cup (125 mL) feta, crumbled

2 eggs, lightly beaten

1/4 tsp (1 mL) *each* salt and black pepper

pinch of nutmeg

1/2 cup (125 mL) melted butter

12 sheets of phyllo pastry

Preheat oven to 375°F (190°C). Bring a pot of salted water to a boil. Add spinach. Simmer for about 3 minutes. Drain, then rinse with cold water. Squeeze out excess water. Heat oil in a saucepan over medium. Add garlic and cook, stirring, until fragrant, about 1 minute. Add onion, spinach, dill and oregano. Cook, stirring occasionally, until onions soften, about 5 minutes. Remove from heat and set aside to cool.

Once cool, add feta, eggs, salt, pepper and nutmeg to the spinach mixture. Mix well and set aside.

Lay one sheet of phyllo on a work surface. Keep remaining phyllo sheets covered with a damp kitchen towel. Cut phyllo sheet lengthwise into 4 strips. Lay one strip lengthwise in front of you. Brush with melted butter. Cover with a second strip of phyllo. Brush with butter. Drop 1 Tbsp (15 mL) spinach mixture in the bottom corner. Fold up diagonally to form a triangle. Keep folding, maintaining the triangular shape until you reach the end of the strip. Repeat with remaining phyllo and filling. Place triangles on a parchment-lined baking sheet. Bake until golden, about 15 minutes. Serve warm or at room temperature with tzatziki on the side for dipping.

2 triangles: 190 Calories; 11 g Total Fat (3 g Mono, 0.5 g Poly, 6 g Sat); 60 mg Cholesterol; 17 g Carbohydrate (1 g Fibre, 2 g Sugar); 6 g Protein; 330 mg Sodium

Place yogurt in a medium bowl. Using the small or medium holes on a box grater, grate the cucumber over the yogurt. Add dill, lemon juice and garlic. Stir together to combine. Season with salt and pepper. Chill at least 1 hour to allow flavours to blend.

3 Tbsp (45 mL): 25 Calories; 2 g Total Fat (0 g Mono, 0 g Poly, 1.5 g Sat); trace Cholesterol; 2 g Carbohydrates; 0 g Fibre; 1 g Sugar; trace Protein; 10 mg Sodium

Pick spinach leaves, as needed, a few at a time from each plant. The flavour tends to deteriorate as the weather heats up and the plant matures and goes to flower.

Tzatziki

1 cup (250 mL) Balkan-style yogurt, well drained

1/2 large seedless cucumber, peeled

3 Tbsp (45 mL) chopped fresh dill

2 Tbsp (30 mL) lemon juice

3 garlic cloves, minced

salt and black pepper to taste

Stuffed Squash Blossoms

Serves 4 as an appetizer

No matter how many squash plants you plant, you are going to be overwhelmed with zucchini or squash, your friends and neighbours will refuse to take any more off your hands, and your freezer will be chock-full of zucchini bread. I'm afraid if you're already at that point, this recipe won't help you, but it does help nip the problem in the bud (actually, a little later than that). Squash blossoms are mild and slightly earthy, with a hint of the flavour of the fruit to come. Harvest the blossoms early in the day before the heat of the sun makes them more fragile. If you prefer not to diminish your later harvest, pick only the male flowers, but if you don't mind sacrificing a few fruits, the female flowers with the small undeveloped squash on one end will be perfectly tender-crisp and add interest to the dish.

6 Tbsp (90 mL) soft goat cheese

2 tsp (10 mL) finely chopped fresh parsley

1 tsp (5 mL) finely chopped fresh basil

1/2 tsp (2 mL) crushed red peppers

12 zucchini or squash blossoms, with stems

vegetable oil, as needed, for frying

1 cup (250 mL) flour

1/4 tsp (1 mL) salt

1 cup (250 mL) cold sparkling water

Combine goat cheese, parsley, basil and crushed red peppers in a small bowl. Mix well.

Gently pull out the pistil or stamen at the centre of each blossom. Holding the blossom open, stuff 2 tsp (10 mL) cheese mixture inside each one. Press gently to spread the cheese inside a little, then twist the ends of the blossoms closed.

Fill a medium saucepan 2 inches (5 cm) deep with oil. Heat until a deep-fat or candy thermometer registers 350°F (175°C).

Stir together flour and salt in a medium bowl. Whisk in sparkling water. Holding the blossoms by the stem, dip into batter to coat, then lay in the oil to fry, cooking no more than 4 blossoms at once. Cook until batter is crisp and light golden, 1 1/2 to 2 minutes. Using a slotted spoon, transfer to paper towels to drain. Salt lightly. Repeat with remaining flowers. Serve immediately.

1 serving: 220 Calories; 10 g Total Fat (4.5 g Mono, 2 g Poly, 2.5 g Sat); 5 mg Cholesterol; 26 g Carbohydrate (2 g Fibre, 1 g Sugar); 7 g Protein; 360 mg Sodium

Zucchini "Noodles" with Balsamic Reduction and Parmesan

Serves 4

This is the way to eat zucchini! The zucchini flavour comes first—it's not hidden by competing ingredients. A few key additions accent its delicacy, making this recipe celebrate the essence of zucchini. Whatever you do, don't bother making this recipe with anything but the freshest (picked the same day, no older), most perfect zucchini (so no giants here—save those for zucchini cake). It doesn't hurt that it's also a near-perfect summer recipe—it requires a minimal amount of prep, and the stove is off again almost before you notice it was ever on.

1 cup (250 mL) balsamic vinegar

6 small-medium (about 6 to 7 inches, 15 to 18 cm, long each) zucchini or summer squash (or a combination), unpeeled

1 Tbsp (15 mL) grape seed oil

3 cloves garlic, minced

1/4 tsp (1 mL) salt

1/2 tsp (2 mL) black pepper

1/4 cup (60 mL) loosely packed fresh Parmesan shavings

1/4 cup (60 mL) loosely packed fresh basil leaves

Bring balsamic vinegar to a simmer in a small saucepan over medium heat. Cook until thick and syrupy and reduced to about 1/3 cup (75 mL), 5 to 10 minutes.

Use a mandoline or a sharp knife to slice zucchini lengthwise about 1/4 inch (6 mm) thick.

Heat oil in a large sauté pan over medium-high. Add zucchini slices, garlic, salt and pepper and cook, stirring, until tender-crisp and lightly golden, about 3 to 4 minutes. Transfer to a serving platter. Sprinkle with parmesan shavings and drizzle with balsamic reduction. Tear basil leaves into medium-sized pieces and scatter overtop.

1 serving: 150 Calories; 6 g Total Fat (1.5 g Mono, 3 g Poly, 1.5 g Sat); 5 mg Cholesterol; 19 g Carbohydrate (3 g Fibre, 13 g Sugar); 6 g Protein; 270 mg Sodium

Summer squash are tastiest when picked and eaten young. The more you pick, the more the plants will produce. Cut the fruit cleanly from the plant, and avoid damaging the leaves and stems to prevent disease and insect problems.

Pumpkin Crème Brûlée

Serves 4

There's something so endearing about the way a pumpkin plant sprawls through the garden that many of us will find a space for a plant or two, no matter what. Some varieties, especially the larger pumpkins, are best suited for jack-o'-lantern carving, but others are quite tasty—don't believe anyone who says canned pumpkin purée is tastier than that made from home-grown pumpkins. This recipe can easily be doubled, tripled or more to serve a larger group.

1 medium pumpkin

1 1/2 cups (375 mL) heavy cream

1/2 cup (125 mL) homogenized milk

1/4 tsp (1 mL) cinnamon

1/8 tsp (0.5 mL) nutmeg

pinch *each* ginger and ground cloves

4 egg yolks

1/2 cup (125 mL) granulated sugar

1/4 cup (60 mL) coarse sugar

Preheat oven to 350°F (175°C). Slice off the bottom of the pumpkin to make it sit flat, then cut the stem end off. Using a large knife, cut off all the skin. Cut pumpkin in half or quarters. Scrape out the seeds and pulp with a spoon. Place pumpkin pieces in a baking dish and add water to cover the bottom of the dish. Bake until the flesh is tender and pierces easily with a fork, 45 minutes to an hour or more. Drain off any remaining liquid and set pumpkin aside to cool. Purée in a food processor until smooth. Set aside.

Preheat oven to 300°F (150°C). Heat cream, milk, cinnamon, nutmeg, ginger and cloves in a medium saucepan over medium, stirring occasionally. Remove from heat and set aside to infuse for about 15 minutes.

Meanwhile, beat egg yolks in a large bowl. Add sugar and whisk until aerated and slightly paler yellow. Pour in cream mixture in a thin stream, whisking constantly. Add 1/4 cup (60 mL) pumpkin purée and whisk thoroughly (reserve remaining puree for another use). Divide mixture evenly among 4 oven-proof ramekins or teacups. Place in a larger

pan and add hot water to at least halfway up the sides. Bake on the centre rack of the oven until almost set (the custards should still wiggle a little in the middle when you shake the pan), 30 to 40 minutes. Remove from the water bath and set aside to cool at room temperature, about 15 minutes. Cover ramekins with plastic wrap (make sure the wrap does not touch the surface of the custard). Transfer to refrigerator to chill at least 2 hours and up to 24 hours.

To serve, first unwrap custards. Sprinkle 2 Tbsp (30 mL) sugar evenly over the surface of each. Arrange on a baking sheet. Either broil until sugar is browned and bubbling, 1 to 2 minutes, or caramelize it with a kitchen torch. Cool 1 minute before serving.

1 serving: 370 Calories; 22 g Total Fat (7 g Mono, 1.5 g Poly, 13 g Sat); 275 mg Cholesterol; 41 g Carbohydrate (trace Fibre, 39 g Sugar); 5 g Protein; 40 mg Sodium

Strawberry and Cream-filled Chocolate Crepes

Serves 4

Now that strawberries are readily available year-round, they can seem almost commonplace. But home-grown strawberries are a world apart from the overgrown, tasteless imposters so often found in stores. Strawberries from the garden are smaller, but fragrant and bursting with flavour, tasting of summer breezes and flowers. What better way to start a summer weekend than with strawberries fresh from the garden for breakfast? This recipe dresses them up, but only barely, and that's all they need.

2/3 cup (150 mL) flour

1/4 cup (60 mL) cocoa

pinch of salt

1 egg

2 Tbsp (30 mL) superfine sugar

1 1/2 cups (375 mL) milk, *divided*

2 Tbsp (30 mL) butter, *divided*

2 1/2 cups (625 mL) sliced strawberries

1 1/2 cups (375 mL) whipped cream

confectioner's sugar, for dusting

Preheat oven to 275°F (140°C) and put a plate in to warm.

Sift together flour, cocoa and salt into a large bowl. Make a well in the centre. In a separate medium bowl, combine egg, sugar and 3/4 cup (175 mL) milk. Whisk until well combined. Pour into well in flour mixture. Whisk, slowly drawing more of the dry mixture in from the sides. Beat in remaining milk. Transfer to a pitcher.

Warm a medium non-stick sauté pan or a crepe pan over medium heat. Add 1 tsp (5 mL) butter. Once the butter has melted, pour in enough batter to just cover the bottom. Tilt the pan to swirl the batter around, making a thin, even layer. Cook until the edges begin to dry and lift away from the pan, about 30 seconds. Flip gently with a spatula. Cook the other side until golden, about 30 seconds more. Transfer to the warmed plate, top with a round of parchment paper and keep warm in the oven. Cook remaining batter in the same way, adding additional butter to the pan as necessary, and separating crepes with parchment paper (otherwise they'll stick together).

When ready to serve, lay crepes one at a time on plates. Top each crepe with about 1/4 cup (60 mL) sliced strawberries in a line down the centre, then roll the crepe around it. Top with a few more strawberries, a dollop of cream and a dusting of confectioner's sugar.

1 serving: 360 Calories; 20 g Total Fat (6 g Mono, 1 g Poly, 12 g Sat); 115 mg Cholesterol; 39 g Carbohydrate (4 g Fibre, 16 g Sugar); 10 g Protein; 135 mg Sodium

Strawberry Shortcake Revisited

Serves 4

Sometimes with something as good as strawberries from your own garden, less is more. On the other hand, sometimes it's not. This dish brings back familiar memories of strawberry shortcake, but it's in a whole different league. Tender, only mildly sweet biscuits infused with lemon flavour replace the sweet sponge cake, mascarpone cheese adds tangy richness to the whipped cream, and the strawberries' floral nature is emphasized by the basil. This is, simply put, a bit of a show-off dish.

1 1/2 cups (375 mL) flour

1/2 cup (125 mL) cornmeal

2/3 cup (150 mL) plus 2 tsp (10 mL) sugar, *divided*

2 tsp (10 mL) baking powder

2 tsp (10 mL) lemon zest

1/2 tsp (2 mL) salt

6 1/2 Tbsp (97 mL) butter, chilled and cut into small pieces

1 egg

4 tsp (20 mL) lemon juice

1/4 cup (60 mL) whole milk, plus more for brushing

(see next page)

Preheat oven to 375°F (190°C), with the rack in the top third of the oven.

Combine flour, cornmeal, 2/3 cup (150 mL) sugar, baking powder, lemon zest and salt in the bowl of a food processor (or a medium bowl). Add butter and process in short bursts (or cut in with pastry cutter) until the mixture resembles coarse meal.

Combine egg and lemon juice in a small bowl. Add to flour mixture. Process in short bursts (or stir) until the mixture starts to form clumps. Add 1/4 cup (60 mL) milk and process (or stir) just until dough comes together. Add more milk if necessary for dough to hold.

Drop in 8 roughly equal rounds on a parchment-lined baking sheet. Brush tops with milk. Sprinkle with remaining 2 tsp (10 mL) sugar. Bake until golden and a skewer inserted into the centre of a biscuit comes out clean. Transfer to a rack to cool. Can be made 1 day ahead.

Place strawberries in a medium bowl. Add basil and drizzle vodka overtop. Toss gently to combine; set aside for 30 minutes to macerate.

Meanwhile, whip cream to soft peaks. Add vanilla and whip to stiff peaks. Gently fold in mascarpone.

Place 1 biscuit on each of 4 plates. Top with a dollop of mascarpone mixture, then some of the strawberries and their juices. Add a second biscuit on top, a little more mascarpone, and more strawberries with their juices. Serve immediately.

1 serving: 830 Calories; 47 g Total Fat (7 g Mono, 1.5 g Poly, 30 g Sat); 195 mg Cholesterol; 88 g Carbohydrate (3 g Fibre, 41 g Sugar); 12 g Protein; 620 mg Sodium

1 1/2 cups (375 mL) sliced strawberries

2 Tbsp (30 mL) lime vodka

1/4 cup (60 mL) basil chiffonade (see p. 15)

1/2 cup (125 mL) whipping cream

1/2 tsp (2 mL) vanilla

1 cup (250 mL) mascarpone cheese

Roasted Sunchokes with Hazelnuts

Serves 4

Sunchokes suffer from a bit of an identity crisis. You may be more familiar with the name "Jerusalem artichokes," but when Samuel de Champlain sent the fist samples to France from Québec in the 1600s, he dubbed them *patates du Canada,* or Canadian potatoes. The name sunchoke has become more popular of late; it is closer to the aboriginal name for the plant, which translates to English as "sun root." No matter what you call them, they're delightful. They can be eaten raw and are nice and crunchy this way, but a little bland. Once they hit the heat, they become more appealing: tender-crisp, with an earthy, nutty flavour that bears some similarities to that of artichokes. They'll add complex flavour to soups or stews and are delicious in simpler preparations, pan-fried or roasted, as here. Take care not to overcook them—it can happen quickly, and they can become tough and mealy.

2 cups (500 mL) cool water

1/2 lemon

2 lbs (900 g) sunchokes

2 Tbsp (30 mL) grape seed oil

2 Tbsp (30 mL) chopped fresh rosemary

1 Tbsp (15 mL) chopped fresh thyme

1 tsp (5 mL) salt

2 tsp (10 mL) black pepper

2 Tbsp (30 mL) coarsely chopped hazelnuts

2 Tbsp (30 mL) hazelnut oil

Preheat oven to 375°F (190°C). Place water in a medium bowl. Squeeze juice from the lemon into the water, and add the lemon half.

Scrub, but do not peel sunchokes, then slice crosswise into 1/2 inch (12 cm) thick pieces. As you slice them, transfer immediately to the bowl of lemon water (they oxidize very quickly). Drain and dry as much as possible on paper towels. Dry the bowl and return sunchokes to bowl. Drizzle grape seed oil over top; add rosemary, thyme, salt and pepper. Toss to coat. Transfer to a baking sheet and cook for 5 minutes. Add hazelnuts and stir to distribute evenly. Return to oven and roast until golden and just tender, about 5 minutes more. Transfer to a serving dish and drizzle with hazelnut oil. Serve immediately.

1 serving: 340 Calories; 16 g Total Fat (6 g Mono, 8 g Poly, 1.5 g Sat); 0 mg Cholesterol; 40 g Carbohydrate (4 g Fibre, 0 g Sugar); 6 g Protein; 590 mg Sodium

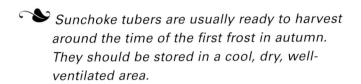 *Sunchoke tubers are usually ready to harvest around the time of the first frost in autumn. They should be stored in a cool, dry, well-ventilated area.*

Seared Strip Loin with Classic Béarnaise Sauce

Serves 4

Tarragon brings a heady licorice flavour to any dish. It's a natural with seafood, poultry and eggs, or snipped into a vinaigrette. French tarragon has more flavour than the Russian variety and is what's called for in most recipes. If you grow only Russian tarragon, you'll need to use about 1 1/2 times as much as is called for in the recipe, and the finished flavour will be less complex and tart. Tarragon can be overpowering—it's not called the dragon herb for nothing. Béarnaise sauce is a classic with steak or seafood (but it's also delicious in place of its cousin, Hollandaise, with eggs Benedict), and the tarragon vinegar it uses is a great way to preserve the herb for a variety of dishes.

4 x 1 inch (2.5 cm) thick strip loin steaks (about 8 oz, 225 g, *each*)

1 Tbsp (15 mL) grape seed oil

1 1/2 tsp (7 mL) *each* salt and black pepper

1/2 cup (125 mL) tarragon vinegar (see opposite)

1/4 cup (60 mL) minced shallots

2 Tbsp (30 mL) finely chopped fresh tarragon, *divided*

3 egg yolks

1 Tbsp (15 mL) finely chopped fresh parsley

1/2 cup (125 mL) clarified butter

lemon juice, to taste

dash of hot pepper sauce

Bring steaks to room temperature and pat dry with paper towel. Heat a large heavy sauté pan over medium. Rub steaks on both sides with oil, then sprinkle with 1 tsp (5 mL) salt and pepper. Cook steaks about 4 minutes on each side, turning once, for medium-rare. Transfer to a plate and tent loosely with foil. Set aside.

For the sauce, combine tarragon vinegar, shallots and 1 Tbsp (15 mL) tarragon in a small heavy saucepan. Bring to a simmer over medium-high, then cook until no liquid remains (the shallot mixture will still be moist, but no excess liquid should remain in the pan).

Place egg yolks in a small heat-proof bowl. Whisk in shallot mixture. Set bowl over a small saucepan of simmering water. Cook, whisking constantly, until yolks have thickened and lightened in colour, 4 to 5 minutes (be careful not to scramble the yolks). Remove from heat. Add parsley and remaining 1 Tbsp (15 mL) tarragon. Very slowly drizzle in clarified butter, whisking constantly. Whisk in lemon juice, hot pepper sauce, and remaining 1/2 tsp (2 mL) salt and pepper. Serve steaks with Béarnaise on the side.

1 serving: 760 Calories; 67 g Total Fat (24 g Mono, 5 g Poly, 32 g Sat); 330 mg Cholesterol; 9 g Carbohydrate (2 g Fibre, 1 g Sugar); 31 g Protein; 630 mg Sodium

Tarragon Vinegar

2 cups (500 mL) red or white wine vinegar

1/2 cup (125 mL) lightly packed fresh tarragon leaves

2 to 3 sprigs of tarragon, for garnish

Lightly roll the tarragon leaves between your hands to bruise slightly. Place in a sterile glass jar.

Bring vinegar to a boil in a small saucepan. Remove from heat and pour into jar over tarragon. Cool to room temperature, then cover. Set aside in a sunny place for about 2 weeks. After the first week, taste every other day or so; when it has reached the desired strength, strain vinegar off into a fresh sterile jar, discarding solids. Add fresh tarragon sprigs to the jar for garnish, if desired. Cover and keep refrigerated.

1/4 cup (60 mL): 20 Calories; 0 g Total Fat (0 g Mono, 0 g Poly, 0 g Sat); 0 mg Cholesterol; 4 g Carbohydrate (2 g Fibre, 0 g Sugar); 0 g Protein; 40 mg Sodium

Thyme and Tomato Fondue with Grilled Rib-eye

Serves 4

Commercially grown fresh thyme in grocery stores can be a little bit insipid; garden-grown thyme, on the other hand, is lush and flavourful, and I've never seen the exquisite lemon variety in a grocery store. Thyme blends well with others herbs and helps bring together different elements of a dish. It pairs particularly well with onions, tomatoes, potatoes, eggs and meat. Don't limit this fondue to topping steaks—it's great with poultry and fish or added to a sandwich.

1 cup (250 mL) shallots, peeled and halved or quartered if large

1 Tbsp (15 mL) grape seed oil

2 cups (500 mL) loosely packed oven-dried tomatoes (see Tip)

3 Tbsp (45 mL) chopped fresh thyme

1/2 tsp (2 mL) salt

1 tsp (5 mL) black pepper

1/4 cup (60 mL) extra virgin olive oil

4 x 1 inch (2.5 cm) thick rib-eye steaks

1 Tbsp (15 mL) grape seed oil

1 tsp (5 mL) *each* salt and black pepper

Preheat oven to 300°F (150°C). Toss shallots with grape seed oil and spread in a single layer in a pie plate. Roast until soft and golden around the edges, about 35 to 40 minutes. Set aside to cool to room temperature.

Cut the tomatoes crosswise into 1 inch (2.5 cm) pieces and place in a medium bowl. Add shallots, thyme, salt and pepper and mix. Drizzle olive oil over and stir to coat.

Preheat grill to medium-high. Bring steaks to room temperature and pat dry with paper towel. Rub steaks on both sides with oil, then sprinkle both sides with salt and pepper. Grill for about 4 to 5 minutes on each side for medium-rare, or to desired doneness. Transfer to a plate and tent loosely with foil. Set aside to rest 5 minutes before serving. Serve topped with a generous portion of thyme and tomato fondue.

1 serving: 750 Calories; 59 g Total Fat (29 g Mono, 8 g Poly, 18 g Sat); 110 mg Cholesterol; 36 g Carbohydrate (4 g Fibre, 14 g Sugar); 36 g Protein; 1510 mg Sodium

Tip

To make oven-dried tomatoes, preheat your oven to 225°F (110°C). Halve lengthwise as many smallish Roma-type tomatoes as you like and squeeze out and discard the seeds (it's fine if a few seeds stick to the walls, as long as you get rid of most of them). Lay the tomatoes cut side up in a single layer on a parchment-lined baking sheet; pack them tightly together, if necessary

Place in the oven to dry for 4 to 8 hours. Check them occasionally; you may want to move some of the tomatoes from the outer edges to the centre of the tray, or if cooking more than one tray at a time, rotate them on the racks. When the tomatoes are done, they should be fairly dry to the touch, but not browned, about half as dry as dry-packed sun-dried tomatoes. Remove from oven and cool to room temperature. Cover and refrigerate up to 1 week; place in a jar and cover with olive oil to refrigerate up to 2 weeks; or package in freezer bags and freeze up to 6 months.

Panzanella

Serves 4

No matter how much I plan to restrain myself each year, or how many other things I'd like to grow more of, I can't resist tomatoes. The sheer variety is what really does me in—how could I not grow at least one Black Krim, one Eva's Purple Ball, one Lemon Boy, one Juliet, one Tiny Tim, one Brandywine, on and on and on, and before you know it, my garden is at least half occupied by tomatoes. This salad is a great way to show off a few varieties of tomatoes. Because it is so simple, it hides nothing; it will be exactly as tasty (or not) as what you put into it. So don't skimp—you need a really great, fragrant loaf of bread, a fantastic olive oil, perfectly ripe tomatoes from the garden, a fresh, crisp cuke and flavourful basil.

1/2 loaf ciabatta or crusty Italian bread, sliced 3/4 inch (2 cm) thick

1/2 cup (125 mL) extra virgin olive oil, *divided*

2 cups (500 mL) tomatoes, left whole, cut in half or wedges, depending on size

1 medium seedless cucumber, cut into bite-sized pieces

1 small red onion, thinly sliced

3/4 cup (175 mL) loosely packed fresh basil leaves, torn

1/2 tsp (2 mL) salt

1 tsp (5 mL) black pepper

1 Tbsp (15 mL) red wine vinegar

Preheat grill to medium. Lightly brush bread slices on both sides with olive oil. Grill until crispy on the outside and nicely grill-marked, about 2 minutes on each side. Remove from heat and cut into bite-sized pieces.

Combine tomatoes, cucumber, onion, basil, salt and pepper in a large bowl. Add bread. Drizzle 3 Tbsp (45 mL) olive oil over, then toss to combine well. Set aside at room temperature to combine flavours for about an hour.

Just before serving, toss in 1 Tbsp (15 mL) vinegar. Taste and adjust seasoning to your liking with vinegar, olive oil, salt and pepper. Serve immediately.

1 serving: 370 Calories; 29 g Total Fat (22 g Mono, 2.5 g Poly, 4 g Sat); 0 mg Cholesterol; 27 g Carbohydrate (3 g Fibre, 5 g Sugar); 5 g Protein; 340 mg Sodium

Keep tomato plants evenly moist to encourage good fruit production. Except for the very small bush selections, tomatoes tend to be quite tall and are prone to flopping over unless stakes, wire hoops, tomato cages or other supports are used. Pick the fruit as soon as it is ripe. Tomatoes pull easily from the vine with a gentle twist when they are ready for picking.

Smoked Tomato Sauce with Prawns and Angel Hair Pasta

Serves 4

This tomato sauce is extremely versatile—omit the prawns and use with other seafood or poultry pasta dishes; leave out the red pepper flakes for a mellower sauce. The smoked tomatoes add complex flavour, but if you're pressed for time and need an extra-quick tomato sauce, skip the smoking process for a sauce that's done in under 15 minutes. Once you try smoking tomatoes, you'll find myriad of uses for them; try them in soups, sauces, sandwiches, even salad dressing.

1/4 cup (60 mL) extra virgin olive oil

4 cloves garlic, minced, *divided*

1 1/2 tsp (7 mL) red pepper flakes

1/2 tsp (2 mL) salt

smoked tomatoes (see opposite), cut in half again lengthwise

1 tsp (5 mL) sugar

black pepper to taste

1 Tbsp (15 mL) basil chiffonade (see p. 15)

zest from 1 lemon

1 tsp (5 mL) grape seed oil

2 tsp (10 mL) butter

2 tsp (10 mL) lemon juice

1 lb (454 g) prawns, peeled and deveined

3/4 lb (340 g) angel hair pasta

Combine olive oil, 3/4 of the garlic, red pepper flakes and salt in a medium saucepan. Heat over medium-high, stirring, until fragrant, about 30 to 45 seconds (you don't want to brown the garlic). Add tomatoes and sugar, bring to a simmer and cook, stirring occasionally, about 7 minutes. Use a hand blender (or transfer to a blender) to purée until smooth. Stir in pepper, basil and lemon zest and check seasoning.

Heat grape seed oil and butter in a sauté pan over medium. Add remaining garlic and cook, stirring, until fragrant. Add prawns and lemon juice and cook, stirring, until pink and opaque throughout, 3 to 7 minutes, depending on size.

Meanwhile, bring a large pot of salted water to a boil. Add pasta and cook, stirring, until al dente, 3 to 4 minutes. Drain. Toss with sauce and prawns and serve immediately.

The sauce will keep, covered and refrigerated, up to 1 week, or frozen up to 2 months.

1 serving: 360 Calories; 21 g Total Fat (12 g Mono, 3 g Poly, 4 g Sat); 175 mg Cholesterol; 47 g Carbohydrate (7 g Fibre, 17 g Sugar); 37 g Protein; 490 mg Sodium

Tip

To make smoked tomatoes, soak 2 cups (500 mL) apple, alder or hickory wood chips in 4 cups (1 L) water for at least an hour. Meanwhile, prepare an ice water bath and bring a large saucepan of water to a rolling boil. Hull 2 1/2 lbs (1.1 kg) Roma tomatoes tomatoes and cut an X in the blossom end. Working in batches if necessary, drop the tomatoes into the water. Once the water returns to a boil, cook for about 30 seconds, then transfer to the ice water bath. Once cool enough to handle, slip the skins off the tomatoes and discard. Cut tomatoes in half lengthwise; squeeze out and discard the seeds.

Build a fire in your charcoal grill; once the fire is dying out, but there are still some red embers, drain the wood chips and add directly to the fire. Alternatively, preheat your gas grill to low. Drain the wood chips and place in a foil roasting pan directly on the gas flame. Place tomatoes on the grill and shut the lid. Vents, if you have them, should be opened halfway. For a gas grill, turn off the flame after about 15 minutes. Smoke tomatoes for 30 to 45 minutes.

Turnip Gratin with Smoked Gruyère

Serves 4 to 6

Turnips are among the easiest of vegetables to grow in the garden. They're undemanding of the gardener but bountiful in production, and every part of them is edible. The greens can be treated like many others, tossed into salad, wilted or braised on the stove, and the roots can be enjoyed in almost every way: grated raw into salads, in soups and stews, pan-fried or roasted. They'll bring a bit of bite wherever they're added, but when cooked by dry methods, they'll add a bit of sweetness, too. Here they are cooked into a classic, hearty gratin, perfect for cold weather, when turnips are at their best and sweetest; the cheese adds a bit of smoke, and the cayenne adds heat for a dish that'll warm you down to your toes.

2 Tbsp (30 mL) butter, melted

2 lbs (900 g) turnips

1 Tbsp (15 mL) chopped fresh thyme, *divided*

1 1/2 tsp (7 mL) salt, *divided*

1/4 tsp (1 mL) cayenne pepper, *divided*

1 cup (250 mL) half-and-half cream (10 percent)

1 cup (250 mL) grated smoked Gruyère

Preheat oven to 350°F (175°C). Pour melted butter into a 12 inch (30 cm) casserole dish or oven-proof sauté pan.

Use a mandoline or a sharp knife to slice turnips as thinly as possible. Arrange 1/3 of the slices in the dish, overlapping them. Sprinkle with 1/3 of the thyme, salt and cayenne. Repeat twice more, making 3 layers. Cover and bake for about 15 minutes. Add cream, cover and return to oven until tender, about 30 minutes. Increase heat to 450°F (230°C), sprinkle cheese over top and bake, uncovered, until golden brown and bubbling, 10 to 15 minutes. Let stand 5 minutes before serving.

1 serving: 260 Calories; 17 g Total Fat (4.5 g Mono, 1 g Poly, 10 g Sat); 55 mg Cholesterol; 17 g Carbohydrate (4 g Fibre, 9 g Sugar); 10 g Protein; 980 mg Sodium

The leaves of turnip plants can be harvested a few at a time from each plant as needed and steamed or added to stir-fries. The roots should be harvested as soon as they are plump, because they have the best flavour and texture when young. Turnips do not keep well when stored.

Grilled Watermelon Salad with Mint Vinaigrette

Serves 4

Watermelons are difficult to grow in most of Canada, which only makes you appreciate the melons you do get all the more. I often wonder if the watermelons grown in my garden really taste that much better than store-bought or if it's only because I worked so hard to produce them. It's probably a little bit of both. It doesn't hurt that the homegrown ones also produce solid black seeds, perfect for spitting. If you don't grow your own, how will your children or grandchildren get to experience the exquisite joy of watching a black seed sail through the air? Though watermelon is one of my favourite foods, it's only in the last several years that I've considered doing things with it other than just eating as much as I can. It's a great addition to salads, and goes especially well with salty and briny flavours. But you absolutely must try it grilled. Don't worry, it doesn't really get cooked, and stays cool and crisp in the middle, but the outside, where it touches the grill, gets ever so slightly caramelized and smoky.

3 Tbsp (45 mL) extra virgin olive oil

1 Tbsp (15 mL) white wine vinegar

2 Tbsp (30 mL) chopped fresh mint

zest from 1 lemon

salt and black pepper to taste

36 x 1 inch (2.5 cm) cubes watermelon (about 3 cups, 750 mL)

12 bamboo skewers, soaked in cold water for 20 minutes

6 oz (170 g) aged, dry goat cheese, cut into 3/4 inch (2 cm) cubes (24 cubes, total)

24 oven-dried tomatoes (see p. 149)

2 cups (500 mL) arugula

Preheat grill to medium-high. Combine olive oil, vinegar, mint, lemon zest, salt and pepper in a small bowl and mix well.

Pat watermelon dry with paper towels. Thread the skewers with a piece of watermelon, a piece of cheese, a tomato, another piece of watermelon, cheese, tomato, and finish with one last piece of watermelon. Centre the cubes on the skewers so the cheese won't touch the grill and melt.

Place skewers on lightly greased grill and cook, just until grill-marked on opposite sides, about 1 minute on each side.

Toss arugula with half the vinaigrette and divide among 4 plates. Place 3 skewers on each plate and drizzle with remaining vinaigrette. Serve immediately.

1 serving: 260 Calories; 20 g Total Fat (10 g Mono, 1 g Poly, 5 g Sat); 20 mg Cholesterol; 13 g Carbohydrate (2 g Fibre, 10 g Sugar); 10 g Protein; 170 mg Sodium

Watermelon plants like plenty of water during the growth and early fruiting stages but, to intensify the flavour, should be allowed to dry out a bit once the fruit is ripening. A watermelon is generally ready to be picked when the pale white area on the skin, where the fruit sits, turns yellow. Some experimentation may be required before you become adept at judging the ripeness of the fruit.

Index

ABOUT THE AUTHORS

Jennifer Sayers is a chef and writer who has been cooking professionally for over 20 years—although she started in the kitchen long before that. She is passionate about fresh, local ingredients and believes that cooking and eating with the seasons enhances our enjoyment of food.

James Darcy brings a wealth of food experience to the table. He is a self-confessed epicure whose food and travel interests have taken him to tables around the world in France, Italy and Greece as well as Argentina and Borneo.

ABOUT THE PHOTOGRAPHER

Sandy Weatherall, owner of Jinsei Photographics, has been a professional photographer since 1989. She enjoys all areas of photography, but "has a special passion for capturing the visual beauty of good food. After all, we eat with our eyes first!"